THE RETREAT FROM TOLERANCE
A Snapshot of Australian Society

THE RETREAT FROM TOLERANCE
A Snapshot of Australian Society

Edited by
PHILLIP ADAMS

**JOHN BUCHANAN / MARY KALANTZIS
MARCIA LANGTON / CATHARINE LUMBY
DAVID MARR / MEAGHAN MORRIS
McKENZIE WARK**

ABC
BOOKS

This publication is assisted by the Australia Council, the
Australian Government's arts funding and advisory body.

Published by ABC Books for the
AUSTRALIAN BROADCASTING CORPORATION
GPO Box 9994 Sydney NSW 2001

National Library of Australia
Cataloguing-in-Publication entry
The retreat from tolerance: a snapshot of Australian society.

ISBN 0 7333 05512

1. Toleration. 2. Discrimination–Australia. 3.   Australia–Social conditions–
1990– . I. Adams, Phillip, 1939–   . II. Australian Broadcasting
Corporation.

303.380994

Designed by Jim Shepherd
Set in 11/14pt Janson by
Midland Typesetters, Maryborough, Victoria
Printed and bound in Australia by
Australian Print Group, Maryborough, Victoria

5 4 3 2 1

Contents

Introduction

BY PHILLIP ADAMS

> *Intolerance is the* 'DO NOT TOUCH' *sign on something that cannot bear touching. We do not mind having our hair ruffled, but we will not tolerate any familiarity with the toupee that covers our baldness.*
> Eric Hoffer

'Hanson is old news'. Behold an article of faith amongst journalists and pundits. If only. This assessment suggests that they're bored with her and the debate—or, alternatively, that they can't cope with it. If it's boredom rather than defeatism, then this reaction to the Pauline Hanson phenomenon signifies a degree of acceptance. Of acquiescence. It suggests that people are accommodating it and her, that we've taken bigotry on board. Isn't that what's happened in the past, with issues like police corruption and media ownership? Let us hope that intolerance doesn't become just another social atrocity that we decide to live with. Let us hope that this issue isn't over, that this is a story with legs.

Not since the Whitlam victory of 1972 has an election result had such a powerful impact on social mores and political outcomes. What are the ingredients in this sea change? Spontaneous combustion in the electorate? Politicians taking ideological instructions from a U.S.—specifically Republican—example? A new agenda driven by zealots in the Lyons Forum? A capitulation to the old-style religion of Senator Harradine, the Tasmanian tail that wags the mainland dog? A political dynamic generated by opportunism and weekly bursts of market research? Had Keating's arrogance, applauded by the press gallery and the chattering classes, silenced dissent? Had those 'forces of political correctness' intimidated other views and voices? Are we simply seeing the swing of the political pendulum? Did umpteen years of Labor government create tensions like the subterranean pressures along a fault line? Had the High Court exceeded its authority over the parliamentary process?

Is the phenomenon a consequence of a prolonged economic crisis leading to feelings of dispossession in the middle-class? Or an inevitable reaction to the pace of social and technological change? Are the escalating anxieties about Asian immigration just an echo of the old fears about the Yellow Peril—or are they a reaction to the growing realisation that white people may no longer be in control of the planet? Has bigotry been waiting, like anthrax spores in the soil, for a combination of factors that permit an epidemic?

Clearly we're dealing with a complex equation, but I'll be arguing that something else is going on as well. That the Hanson phenomenon is as significant in its way as the Chamberlain phenomenon, and that there may be linkages between the two of them. No, not that Hanson is a victim in the way Chamberlain was a victim—but that both phenomena involved tapping into deep, inchoate feelings within ourselves and our community.

> *In every age of transition men are never so firmly bound to one way of life as when they are about to abandon it, so that fanaticism and intolerance reach their most intense forms just before tolerance and mutual acceptance come to be the natural order of things.*
>
> Bernard Levin

While we cling to the idea of tolerance like mussels to a pier, our attachment is quite a recent one. The 'black armband view of history' may be deplored in Canberra, but a host of Australians recognise that we have a proud tradition of bigotry extending beyond our tragic treatment of an indigenous people to the wider world—a tradition that we've only recently opted to renounce. In a belated attempt to seek redemption for our catastrophic impact on Aboriginal communities—including the slaughter, in massacres and isolated murders, of tens of thousands, not to mention the small matter of the White Australia Policy—Australians had begun to embrace tolerance as the nation's *raison d'être*.

In 1995 I was appointed to the Council of Australian Governments Committee on the Centenary of Federation. An odd mixture of federal, state and territory appointees, we found it hard to agree on the weather, yet, finally, signed off on a report making a series of recommendations on how Australia should celebrate its hundredth birthday.

We heard submissions from the premiers, chief ministers and people representing the alphabet soup of Australian organisations, from the CWA to the RSL. And it became our custom to ask people to describe, to attempt to define, what it meant to be an Australian. People struggled with the notion of Australianness like members of a Christian congregation trying to explain the intricacies of the Holy Trinity. Nobody evoked the Constitution. But then, nobody seemed to have read it. Nor were there ringing endorsements of the monarchy. Just a prevailing view that the Republic was inevitable, if not desirable, and that we should sign off on the issue and get on with the rest of our lives. This advocacy usually fell short of enthusiasm, let alone of passion.

However, finally, and repeatedly, people spoke proudly about Australia's physical presence—while praising to the high heavens above Uluru our recently minted tolerance. Australia was an ancient and beautiful country and the exhilarating idea of tolerance made us, it seemed, an admirable people.

I've heard David Malouf suggest that Australians think of their national identity in terms of trees and landscapes— and the COAG's submissions proved him right. Our far horizons and our jewelled sea, *à la* Dorothea Mackellar, the familiar chiaroscuro of drought and flood, the sense of an ancient and implacable vastness, is deeply felt and can be powerfully articulated. Yet Australia's claim for spirituality extends beyond reverence for the timeless land. It is made complete by that emphasis on tolerance. You'd have thought Australians had invented it.

As Joan Kirner and I worked on the first draft of the report, we marvelled at the stress on tolerance in virtually every submission. While white Australians expressed an almost aboriginal sense of the metaphysical in the physical, in the geography and geology of the continent, it was this allegedly all-pervading human quality that completed the picture. Tolerance transcended the beauties and the terrors of the wide brown land.

If Australians had such an attraction to tolerance, such a need for it, it wasn't simply because it expiates old guilts. It was because people clearly understood that tolerance was the only glue that could hold the place together. They were aware of living in a nation of unprecedented ethnic and religious complexity and were, it seems, increasingly proud of it. Tolerance, we were given to understand, was the miracle ingredient that would keep Australia ticking over. And apart from its critical importance to national identity and well-being, people saw tolerance as crucial to our regional and international relations. To protect our trade and tourism, we had to display our tolerance to our Asian neighbours.

We were also surprised by the unanimity of views regarding Reconciliation. This seemed to provide further proof of our conversion to tolerance. It showed our commitment to that principle of the 'fair go'. As with the issue of the Republic, there were many who were lukewarm in their support, simply seeing Reconciliation as another inevitability. Nonetheless they supported it. In 2001, as Australia begins its second century, in a new millennium, in a fast-changing world, it was accepted and repeatedly stated that we had to 'sign off on the Aboriginal issue'. And, yes, get on with the rest of our lives.

But I really didn't need the Kirner Committee to convince me that Australia had undergone a considerable transformation since my childhood. There's been, for example, the public reaction to the Mabo judgment. Despite energetic campaigns by conservative politicians and mining companies, eagerly supported by talk-back radio announcers, the public had seemed disinclined to panic. There were no outbreaks of violence in rural centres, no demonstrations in city streets. Indeed, the *Australian* chose the late Eddie Mabo as their Australian of the Year, signifying a profound change in editorial emphasis. I gained the distinct impression that my fellow citizens not only accepted Mabo as a part of the sacred 'fair go', but were proud of it.

So while preparing myself for a conservative victory in the 1996 federal election, I agreed with Paul Keating that the electorate had, to a remarkable extent, accepted the 'big picture' issues and had convinced themselves that intolerance couldn't be tolerated.

Hence my astonishment, and despair, at both the scale and the character of the Coalition's victory. It wasn't just the 25 per cent swing to Hanson in Oxley, or Katter's triumph in Kennedy, or the 76.39 per cent (on a two-party preferred basis) that made Wilson Tuckey the biggest vote-puller in the country. It was the clear trend to tub-thumping, boong-bashing populism. It's instructive to analyse the 40 seats with the highest proportion of Aborigines and Torres Strait Islanders. Prior to the election, Labor held 21 of them, including five of the top ten. Now it holds only seven of the 40, and none of the ten.

And that, of course, was just one of many symptoms of the phenomenon that left pollsters, politicians, pundits and academics gobsmacked.

*There is no prejudice so strong as that which arises
from a fancied exemption from all prejudice.*
William Hazlitt

No sooner had our shiny bright PM returned from making
soothing noises in Asia than he seemed to give the diagonal
nod to Pauline Hanson. By refusing to fan the flames of
moderation, John Howard rekindled his nasty 'immigration
debate' of 1988. And not for the first time he talked about
'political correctness', that bizarre analogy for tolerance, as
though really believing that the debate on issues like race
had been stifled.

Had he averted his gaze from the anti-Asian signs
spray-painted on walls and cars as he was chauffeured along
our freeways in his Comcar? Was he deaf to the bombast
and bigotry that had blasted from the shows of the shock
jocks?

Whether it's the snarls of our neo-Nazi organisations
or the strident racism from certain relics in the RSL, the
voice of the bigot has never been silenced in Australia.
Bigotry was enshrined in our constitution, in our laws.
Bigotry was central to our immigration and foreign policies. When we talk about Australia's future in Asia it's as
well to remember that. Does a society made up of 17
million pale people (less 300,000 beleaguered blacks) have
a future with people whom, until a moment ago, we
regarded as less than human? While we're advised to forget
our past, our Asian neighbours remember it vividly. And
our indigenous people are still living it.

Celebrating its happy hundredth in a few years' time,
Australia was devised as a white man's country, defiantly,
arrogantly white. The *Bulletin* proclaimed on its masthead

'Australia for the white man'. Ours was a nation based on exclusion as we protected our whiteness with policies, *bipartisan* policies, that made apartheid look half-baked.

The first federal Labor platform on 24 January 1900 argued for the total exclusion of coloured and other 'undesirable races'. Sir Edmund Barton, speaking in the House of Reps in the same year, in favour of the notorious 'education test' in the Immigration Restriction Bill, said: 'I do not think the doctrine of equality of man was ever really intended to include racial quality.'

A parliamentarian talks in 1858 on the Chinese Immigration Bill of 1858. 'We are threatened by an overwhelming influx of barbarians, men of low social and mental development and given to the indulgence of vices unfit to be named by a decent man.'

When Dick Casey was appointed Governor of Bengal in 1944, he said: 'I could not have had a worse press before I arrived. They protested to high heaven against an Australian being sent to govern them. "Have we become a colony of Australia? How are we to endure the humiliation of a governor from a country that prohibits Indians from entering it?"'

In 1947, Labor's Arthur Calwell defended the deportation of a Chinese refugee who, he claimed, was not eligible to become a permanent resident of Australia. 'There are many Wongs in the Australian community, but I have to say—and I'm sure that the Honourable Member for Balaclava will not mind me doing so—that "two Wongs don't make a white."'

He was still at it in 1972: 'No red-blooded Australian,' said Arthur, 'wants to see a chocolate-coloured Australian in the 1980s.'

A few months earlier, Gough Whitlam had made the following speech to chocolate-coloured people in Port Moresby: 'All Australians must now realise how damaging and dangerous a reputation Australia's present policies produce. We are a European nation on the fringe of the most populace and deprived coloured nations in the world. What the world sees about Australia is that we have an Aboriginal population with the highest infant mortality rate on Earth, that we've eagerly supported the most unpopular war in modern times on the grounds that Asia should be a battleground of our freedom, that we failed to oppose the sale of arms to South Africa, that the whole world believes that our immigration policy is based on colour, and that we run one of the world's last colonies. We might rightly profess our good intentions, but the combination of such policies leans heavily indeed on the world's goodwill and on Australia's credibility.'

Let us remember that Henry Lawson, author of 'Song of the Republic', died a born-again monarchist. But he never changed his views on Asians, whom he hated, as did most of his energetically patriotic peers. Deeply embedded in our culture, racism can rise like a phoenix—or rather, a vulture—with the slightest encouragement. And with racism comes a host of associated phenomena that we must, yet again, address. Two steps forward? So it had seemed. Now, at the very least, it's one step back.

For generations, Australians saw Asia as a stop-over on their way to Europe, as a place for duty-free shopping and duty-free bonking. Men of ministerial rank would arrive in Asian capitals and demand that embassy officials procure for them. Much was made of the ugly American in our region, but we should never forget there was an even uglier

Australian. We have much to live down—and fortunately a growing number of our expat businessmen know this only too well.

> *No man is prejudiced in favour of a thing knowing it to be wrong. He is attached to it on the belief of its being right.*
>
> Thomas Paine

I've been encouraging people to wear a piece of orange ribbon as a sign of their opposition to racism. Recently 20,000 kids attending a rock concert wore the ribbons, as did the members of the bands entertaining them. And when I addressed the Australian Chamber of Commerce in Hong Kong, having chosen the Hanson phenomenon as my topic, I ran out of ribbons long, long before I'd run out of businessmen wanting to pin them to their lapels alongside their Rotary badges.

Much to the pain of people like Pauline Hanson and Geoffrey Blainey, Asians represent one of our largest immigrant groups. But the development of this situation is not so much driven by idealism as opportunism. Far from fearing the teeming millions of Asia because of what we thought these sub-humans might do to our illustrious standard of living, we now seek their favours, their markets, their know-how. The tables have turned dramatically and we now scramble for the crumbs of the rich man's meal. And we know that the best way to plug into Asian markets is through the diaspora, through the network of friends and relatives that connects the economies of Australia's China Towns with Singapore, with Taiwan, with mainland China.

Now that Mandela is president of South Africa, our

treatment of Aborigines will be seen as indicative of our level of civilisation, of equity, of decency. If we fail that test, it will be used against us. It will not suffice to have scrapped the White Australia Policy, to have increased the incidence of Asian immigration. For we're doing it now for economic self-interest, just as we did when we allowed Chinese coolies in during the gold rush. Or dragged islander people into Australia to cut cane.

Not so long ago we were winning international kudos with the Mabo judgment, now the reaction to Wik may blow Reconciliation to smithereens, and the Sydney Olympics and the centenary of Federation, which will bring the world to Australia, may be overshadowed by rising racial tensions. Already sneers about 'the Aboriginal industry' are driving the best and brightest in Aboriginal leadership from the negotiating tables. If Noel Pearson, Galarrwuy Yunupingu, Lois O'Donoghue or Marcia Langton walk away, it will be a tragedy for both Aboriginal Australia and for the nation. And it will resonate throughout the region, giving our critics evidence of ... of what? Perhaps our recalcitrance.

Anyone who watched the ABC's production of 'Frontier' realises that what we are now hearing are the same arguments mounted against Aborigines, against their culture and their rights to land, as were expressed by the white community at the time of the Myall Creek massacre, one of the many Mai Lais arranged by colonial troops or vigilantes. One hundred and fifty years on, there are people, including powerful people, for whom the argument has not advanced by a minute or a thought. 'Aborigines don't own the land because they don't farm it', said a barrister, defending the Myall Creek butchers who had decapitated women and children. (Decapitation saved ammunition). The same social Darwinian arguments about white supremacy are still trotted out, as fresh as packets of defrosted peas.

> *We are chameleons and our partialities and prejudices*
> *change places with an easy and blessed facility.*
> Mark Twain

Tides turn, pendulums swing. Behold a backlash with many ingredients. These include a renewed enthusiasm for censorship, a revival of homophobia, and involve an escalating attack on such institutions as the ABC, the universities and the High Court. But racism remains at the heart of it.

Economic problems do not sufficiently explain the retreat from tolerance. Clearly they exacerbate the problems of racism, but something deeper and more enduring seems to be at work. Even without the tensions provoked by long-term unemployment, hostilities in human beings spontaneously combust. It seems that any manifestation of 'the other' is enough to encourage us. Before Pauline Hanson divided the nation, Lindy Chamberlain stirred our fears, our nightmares. A medieval urge for witch-burning seemed to reincarnate during that long controversy. And economics had nothing to do with it.

Do hatreds linger, waiting for the right conditions to multiply? If so, right conditions can simply involve permissions, the feeling that the time is right.

This book sets out to examine, from various perspectives, why Australia seems to have made such a sharp right turn from its much vaunted liberalism. A society that proudly proclaimed its tolerance, its pluralism, now has to confront the tenacity, the renewed energies, of bigotry. Not to mention pragmatism. Suddenly we seem to be abandoning even the pretence of concern for human rights, at least when they impinge on trade. And once again the censors, scissors in hand, are chorusing 'click go the shears'.

Revisiting old controversies and battlefields, we see surreal alliances between factions in feminism and traditional conservatives, and those who fought at the barricades in the 1960s are often found in bed in the 1990s with those who see cinema, and other forms of mass media, as marketers of alienation that must be V-chipped or controlled. And the free-and-easy nature of the new technologies, particularly the Internet, are causing *frissons* in high places. How can we protect our children, and ourselves, from electronic sin?

Many who fought against restrictive laws of defamation now join forces with others proposing anti-vilification laws with criminal sanctions. The issues and anxieties cross party lines, defying the usual ideological analysis.

> *Laws alone cannot secure freedom of expression: in order that every man present his views without penalty there must be a spirit of tolerance in the entire population.*
>
> Albert Einstein

There are times when it seems that one of our problems is a growing demand for 'niceness'. For public discourse to wipe its feet before it comes in, to have better manners. It's not only the Prime Minister who would like to live in a society where conflict is kept under control.

Not so long ago I was being booed and heckled at a

multicultural conference—for opposing proposed anti-vil-ification legislation. Apart from restating the usual pieties on free speech (which, by definition, also has to be available to those we dislike or despise), I observed that an increasing number of my fellow citizens seemed intent on eliminating social friction, or at least dulling its pain. 'Thou shalt be nice', long a commandment behind the venetian blinds in the suburbs, was becoming trumpeted in what was left of our civic space.

While some preferred the local anaesthesia of New Age gush, others prescribed legal lubricants to prevent abrasion. I dared to suggest, to an angry audience, that social change can only be brought about by people and ideas rubbing together. If you want to smooth off the jagged edges, people have to argue, conflict. Niceness may be nice but it doesn't seem to get us very far. Those anxious to return to the 1950s should remember that while they were nice, they were also suffocating.

> *Whenever there are great virtues, it's a sure sign something's wrong.*
>
> Bertold Brecht

It seemed to me that the outpouring of grief following Andrew Olle's death was symptomatic of this desire for niceness. First and foremost, Andrew was polite, non-confronting. It's hard to remember anything powerful or provocative that Andrew said. And close friends confessed that they had no idea of his political views. Everyone, none-theless, agreed that Andrew was enormously pleasant, decent and, yes, nice.

These seem to be improbable virtues for a prominent

journalist. They could hardly apply to, for example, a John Pilger or a Christopher Hitchens whose very lack of nice-ness gives them a cutting edge. Yet countless Australians had been reassured by Olle's restraint and good manners. He was loved because of what and who he wasn't. He wasn't aggressive and he wasn't Alan Jones.

(One of the main complaints about Paul Keating was that he wasn't nice. He was vulgar and aggressive in Question Time. If his successor has a passion for anything it seems to be for niceness, for making people feel 'comfort-able'. Sadly this niceness does not extend to current prac-tices in business or government. The business community, as triumphantly ascendant as they were during the 1980s, are playing hardball with very hard balls. Economic ration-alism is now resurgent at every level of government and has never been more brutally, less nicely imposed. Increas-ingly, therefore, the idea of niceness can be interpreted as an instruction to smile sweetly, gratefully, while various Godzillas tromp all over your lives.)

Yet a demand for niceness could be detected in our intellectual life. We were to watch our Ps and Qs in gender issues. We were to tread lightly in areas of race. We were not to be so nasty to Helen Darville. On many topics we were urged to conduct our arguments within approved parameters.

Now, much of this was perfectly in order. Discussions could be robust without being offensive. In a pluralist society people holding alternative views can be, indeed must be, accorded respect. I certainly benefited from scru-tinising my own Ps and Qs, not to mention the other 24 letters, having often unconsciously slipped into, for example, sexist language. Yet now there were times when

I grew impatient with what seemed a lengthening list of rules and protocols.

It was like being back at school again where, of course, what passed for public discourse was stultified by an official language that expressed establishment attitudes to everything from untidy lockers to Anzac Day. From the early days of Christianity to school assemblies at Eltham High, the power brokers have attempted to control agendas and modes of expression. So it was wholly appropriate for groups who'd gained political potency after decades of dispossession to demand that they be treated with a modicum of respect.

Fine. But I was, for example, disturbed by the way the debate on AIDS was being conducted and controlled. AIDS was to be spoken of as HIV/AIDS—even though a significant number of rebellious scientists dispute both the causality of HIV, and even its existence. There were to be no 'AIDS victims', 'innocent' or otherwise. AIDS had to be discussed as equally threatening to everybody in the community—hence the absurdity of the Grim Reaper commercial wherein little girls and elderly ladies in bowling cossies were deemed to be at equal risk with gay men engaging in high-risk sexual encounters.

To suggest, as I did, that in Australia AIDS was unlikely to be a significant threat beyond the gay community—and that the official campaign should focus on the risks of anal intercourse—was to invite massive retaliation, not only from gay groups but from the Department of Health.

(It is fascinating to recall that the Department's propaganda material avoided referring to anal sex at all. The one established transmission mode was ignored. And obviously the issue wasn't coyness—oral sex, not believed to pose a significant risk, was invariably discussed.)

One could understand the desire of the gay community to prevent the wave of homophobia we'd observed in the United States. But as surely as the debate on Middle Eastern politics is circumscribed by an ever-vigilant Jewish lobby, AIDS became an area where public discussion was inhibited. In my view it still is.

It is undeniable that political correctness had its impact on certain issues—and on the toffy end of the media. But it remained ineffective in the wider community. The same broadcasters and tabloid columnists tackled the familiar topics in their familiar way—inviting readers and listeners to aim at the usual targets. Nor were the heavy-hitters of the New Right inhibited in their attacks on, for example, the interlocking issues of land rights and Aboriginal culture. Long before Hanson, Western Mining's Hugh Morgan was the doyen of boong-bashers, blazing away in addresses to the H. R. Nicholls Society and in increasingly reckless press statements. As far as Morgan was concerned, Aboriginal cultural was an oxymoron. Nor was Geoffrey Blainey constrained in his attacks on Asian immigration.

> *One may no more live in the world without picking*
> *up the moral prejudices of the world than will be able*
> *to go to Hell without perspiring.*
>
> H. L. Mencken

I've been fighting bigotry for 50 years.

Does this smack of arrogance? Far from seeking to cast myself in an heroic light, that sentence is a confession. Let me now complete it.

I've been fighting bigotry for 50 years—my own.

I can little see point in publishing another book about the current debate on intolerance unless we face the fact that we're all, more or less, prejudiced. I can see no way to deal with the contagion that's raging in our body politic unless we admit that we're all infected by prejudice or, at least, bear the scars of past infections. While it might be pleasant, even therapeutic, to pillory Pauline and her political patrons, it gets us nowhere.

A few months back I was rattling off one-liners about Hanson with the best of them ('Pauline Hanson has done to Canberra what Charles Manson did to Hollywood' was my favourite contribution), but soon realised that we had to stop treating her, and hers, like aliens. Pauline is one of us, and she speaks to prejudices that have been a part of our national and social lives since the first hours of white settlement—and of our families and inner lives ever since.

> *Tolerance is just a makeshift, suitable for an overcrowded and overheated planet. It carries on when loves gives out, and love generally gives out as soon as we move away from our home and our friends.*
>
> E. M. Forster

Even the word we choose to describe a superior state of mind—tolerance—speaks to our arrogance if not to our prejudice. Tolerance. Toleration. I will tolerate you.

In a country made up of a population of some hundreds of ethnic groups and religions, tolerance actually may not be good enough. We need a bigger 'ask', a more ambitious ambit claim. We must aim at acceptance, and hope for celebration. It's a utopian proposition—at a time when even tolerance, with all its implications of condescension and *noblesse oblige*, seems beyond us.

So let's start by recognising that bigotries abound in the best of us. They lurk in our neurons, their ugliness revealed by every lightning flash of the synapses. They may be vestigial, they may belong to the past, on a par with memories, and our conscious beliefs may have them under firm control (just as a morals crusader may have triumphed over his appetite for sin), but the bigotries of our beginnings, the prejudices that we learnt in the home, in the playground or at Sunday School live on. And one of the reasons that we rush to demonise the likes of Pauline Hanson is because we're ashamed of what we feel, however faintly, within us.

> *To live anywhere in the world today and be against equality because of race or colour, is like living in Alaska and being against snow.*
> William Faulkner

It's 1944 and I'm a five year-old attending East Kew Primary School. My best friend, Johnny Sinclair, is a Roman Catholic and we walk to school together every morning and we go home together every night. But in between times, he's a Catholic and I'm a Proddy. He's a Mick at the school next door and I'm at State School. Though we're a long way from Belfast, we chant 'Catholic dogs stink like frogs jumping off hollow logs' at them, and they chant 'State, State, fulla hate' at us. And I recall the flashes of stark terror I'd feel when I saw the nuns coming out of the door. Mysterious and spectral creatures in their long, black gowns, looking like negatives of ghosts. They frightened me almost as much as, years later, the vampires in Hoyts' horror movies.

At playtime I join a ring of kids jeering at a so-called DP, some poor child who's survived the war in Europe. 'Go back to your own country, you reffo', we yell at him, 'reffo' being contemporary shorthand for refugee. We are, of course, echoing the prejudices expressed by parents. Not that we really need parental prompting for as William Golding and our memories remind us, kids are cruel little buggers, savages ever ready to attack the weak and the vulnerable. Which is why we didn't hesitate to abuse, to taunt, a girl who came to school shoeless and in rags. Valerie wasn't foreign—she was just poor.

Perhaps these visceral responses have something to do with evolution's grand plan. But in that playground, underneath the peppercorns, we made that reffo kid cry. I can still see him reeling within a circle of jeering faces. My feelings were mixed—combining pleasure at being part of the dominant group with shame for what we were doing.

Yet I didn't learn much from the experience. Ten years on I was in a gang that enjoyed brief but exhilarating brawls with Italian kids in the back streets of Collingwood and Clifton Hill. 'Go back to your own country.'

(Mark Twain was right about us being chameleons—within a few months of fighting with the 'wogs', we'd be desperately trying to emulate them. Without even noticing our change of attitude, we started hanging around the Legend Coffee Shop in Bourke Street, ordering cappuccinos from the bloke behind the wondrously plumbed and vesuvian espresso machine, trying to say 'grazie' and 'prego' with more authority than embarrassment. We were, as well, all saving up to buy Vespas or Lambrettas.)

Incidentally, no sooner had we dealt with the reffo in the playground than the same jeering, ugly circle formed around a kid with Down's Syndrome we'd found sitting quietly on a playground swing. Kids like that were called Mongoloids, and the name was almost enough. Despite his bewildered smile and obvious wish to be friendly, we bullied and terrified him. I felt shame then and I feel shame now, 50 years later. Yet when planning the campaign for the International Year of the Disabled Person in the early 1980s I still felt, deep inside me, a primitive response to disability. These days I know how to repress such feelings in a nanosecond. And that's what self-styled progressives do with vestigial prejudice—we censor it savagely, instantly, overlaying it with our more sophisticated, considered response. But we are liars if we deny that old terrors no longer exist.

Towards the end of that International Year, when I thought there was nothing left to shock me, when I thought I'd attained a high level of sophistication in dealing with disability, I visited an institution in Perth where, I was told, somebody wanted to meet me. He was sitting in his wheelchair, staring out a window at the far end of a huge, empty room. He remained in profile to me as I approached. Then, at the last second, he spun the chair around to confront me. And half his head wasn't there. Half of him, from head to toe, had been burnt in a tractor accident. 'I was pinned under it for hours', he told me later, 'unable to escape the fire. So now I've got to live in here because I look like something out of a horror movie. If I go down the street in my wheelchair, people literally scream and jump out of the way.' Society has learnt to adjust to the sight of Stephen J. Hawking but are not ready for this young farmer. He has every right to expect better from us but has learnt to accept our limitations.

Some forms of difference make us angry, condemnatory. Others, because they are intimations of our own mortality, make us deeply afraid.

> *Dogs bark at persons whom they do not know.*
>
> Heraclitus

When I was a kid living in Melbourne, I'd never seen a black face. And I suspect that, half a century on, a majority of Australians have had no direct contact with Aborigines. While there weren't a lot of Aborigines around East Kew, there was, as it happened, one, just one, in the next suburb. He was called, inevitably, Jacky, and supervised the pony rides at the Balwyn Sanctuary, a rather glum zoo containing a few woebegone wombats and wallabies. It was Jacky's job to get brats like me on and off the horses, which he did with surly efficiency. And in return he copped a constant stream of what is now described as racial vilification. This was regarded by the kindergarten vilifiers as simply 'giving cheek'. Yet again, I participated in it, albeit half-heartedly.

The next time I saw 'an Abo' was on Melbourne's Princes Bridge. Not one, but two, playing the gumleaf for passers-by. And for coins. Walking with my Dad, who, being on leave, was in his Army uniform, I was awed at the sight of the poor beggars—literally beggars—in the middle of the white man's city. 'Ignore them', my Dad say, pulling at me, 'they're drunks.' And the linking of the Aborigines with booze, with rejection, with the fact that decent, white people should have absolutely nothing to do with them, began. In the school there were books that told stories about 'little black princesses' and others in which Aborigines were rendered into sentimental little golliwogs. But the prime message was that we should despair of Australia's black people, seeing their inevitable 'dying out' as probably the best thing. This was the compassion of the social Darwinian.

Decades later I was supporting the work of Nugget Coombs and Judith Wright McKinney regarding a Treaty and, more recently, have worked with the likes of Pearson, Langton and O'Donoghue on a variety of issues. I've taken my wireless program to Aboriginal outstations and sat beneath the trees talking about issues of health and justice. Yet there are times when, walking through an Aboriginal camp where every window has been smashed by glue-sniffing kids, where nobody picks up the rubbish, where the fathers are too pissed to bother catching barramundi for malnourished children, I can understand something of what Hanson says she feels. This, despite everything I know about dispossession, about the war that's been waged against Aboriginal people for two long centuries, despite a library groaning with books on indigenous politics.

Men never do evil so completely and cheerfully as when they do it from religious conviction.

Blaise Pascal

Another confession. I visited the death camps in Europe for the first time in the early 1970s, gazing with stupefaction at the mountains of hair, shoes and suitcases, trying to imagine the unimaginable horrors that occurred in these buildings, behind the once-electrified fences. On returning to Australia I wrote a column admitting that, as well as

wanting to identify with the victims, I found myself identifying with the guards. After all, most blue-eyed blondes
were on the other side of the barbed wire.

As a kid I learnt from my father, a Congregational
minister, that Jesus Christ was put to death by the Jews.
I knew enough of anti-Semitism to regard the word 'Jew'
as a pejorative. Anti-Semitism, however, remained the
bigotry of the affluent, the prejudice of the Melbourne
Club, with the working class having more immediate
targets—the Italians and Greeks who wouldn't speak
English, the Chows who put dogs and cats into their
Chinese food. Nonetheless it was only in my early teens,
when I started to get glimmerings about Holocaust, that
I confronted my prejudice.

The fact that I disapprove of Israel's policy towards the
Palestinians and have frequently interviewed the likes of
Edward Said and Hanan Ashwari does not save me from
being described, by the League of Rights and other lunatic
organisations, as a Jewish apologist. While some of my best
friends are, emphatically, Jewish, while I see the Jews as
making a contribution to mankind out of all proportion to
their population (which is a mere one per cent of the
human race), there are still times when I shrink at the
vulgarities of Double Bay culture, summed up in the mem-
orable line of Zero Mostel in *The Producers*: 'If you've got
it, flaunt it'. And there are times when the sight of an Has-
sidic Jew in full regalia recalls my youthful reaction to the
nuns in the Catholic school next door. I sometimes wonder
if my rage with ultra-conservative Jews in Israel, for their
role in the assassination of Yitzhak Rabin, isn't tinged with
vestigial anti-Semitism.

In the late 1950s and early 1960s, prior to the release

of Britain's Wolfenden Report, I campaigned for homosexual law reform. My efforts included attempts to per-
suade the Fabian Society to hold a seminar in Victoria. But
after a number of meetings, at which people's voices always
dropped by several octaves, nothing eventuated. Decades
later, while still defending the love that dare not speak its
name, I remain uncomfortable with the smorgasbord of gay
culture as it Mardi-Gras's its way up Oxford Street and
takes such a dominant position in literature and the arts.
And there are sexual practices that seem to me not merely
dangerous but symptomatic of self-hatred and institutionalised guilt. (I once interviewed an academic who tried to
convince me that fisting was the best possible form of male
bonding. Thanks, but no thanks.)

Whether I'm reacting to Hemingway-style chest-
thumping, Alan Jones's love of Rugby or the heterosexual
nastinesses of the Hell's Angels, I find cultures based on
sexuality tedious. I can no more escape the odd nanosecond
of homophobia than I can regular outbursts of heteropho-
bia provoked by ads for Tooheys, or by Rugby, bike gangs
or, latterly, the gun lobby.

While you're free to regard the responses I fail to
repress as reprehensible, I freely acknowledge them.
Because they enable me to understand what goes on in the
minds of many who are deeply afraid of what they perceive
as the ascendancy, the triumphalism, of homosexual
culture. And I believe that for everyone who cheers at the
Mardi Gras floats, there's someone else who's affronted and
offended by them, whose worst fears are confirmed.
Moreover, amongst those cheering and clapping are many
who are not entirely convinced—whose bigotries might
flare in another context. That's one of the oddest aspects

of our species—that we hold contradictory, mutually exclusive views on so many topics. Whether it's multiculturalism, censorship, voluntary euthanasia or the death penalty, our responses can be unpredictable. It depends on who's pressing our buttons.

I confess because I think we should all confess, believing that we can't begin the many processes of reconciliation until we admit to the things in our social history, in our personal histories, that colour our attitudes. But in confessing I know I'm taking a risk.

I took it once at a meeting in Melbourne where the audience was made up of around 100 of the most decent people I know, a group whose credentials in a score of civil rights battles and social crusades were impeccable. I admired them and, by and large, they seemed fond of me. At the time I was something of a mascot for them, a kid who was publishing in newspaper columns the opinions they'd long held. On this occasion, however, I infuriated them.

'I'm going to read a list of words to you', I said. 'As I read them I want you to feel, and acknowledge, your response. Because I believe that some of you, all of you, will react badly to one or more of them. You will hear them as pejorative terms and will quickly repress that response in alarm and embarrassment. And you'll superimpose your more sophisticated, more reasoned views.'

They were bristling even before I started to read out the list, which included words such as 'Jew', 'Aborigine', 'homosexual', 'communist', 'trade unionist'. (These days you could add terms like 'dole bludger' and 'feminist' to the list.) That these decent people were even angrier afterwards I saw as proof of the proposition—that they'd detected within themselves the emotions I'd foreseen. Not that the point of the exercise was to embarrass them with evidence of their subconscious infamies—any more than the purpose of my confessions is to expiate me from guilt. I remain concerned with two simple truths. First, that we have these feelings. Second, that we can deal with them. We can learn from them.

Come to think of it, I can't think of anything we learn that doesn't involve some pain in the learning. We learn about fire from burnt fingers, about gravity by falling out of trees. Life itself gains intensity from one's growing awareness of death.

Censorship doesn't work. Denial doesn't help. Anti-vilification legislation won't solve the problem. And demonising our opponents as 'rednecks' won't be a whole lot of help.

Please don't laugh, but I think it's important to engage the entire community, or as much of it as we can reach, in a series of serious discussions. Because I concur with the views of Pablo Casals who, on his eightieth birthday announced: 'The situation is hopeless—we must take the next step.' The next step may not be as difficult as we imagine.

As a novice talk-back announcer I learnt a significant lesson—that vehemence of expression does not necessarily equate with depth of conviction. I would find my board lit up with callers who were on intimate terms with colleagues such as John Laws and Alan Jones—bursting to recycle views on Aborigines, homosexuals, trade unionists, Vietnamese and Cambodians. I had two obvious choices: I could take the calls and proceed to insult them; or I could look at the screen and select callers more to my liking.

Instead, I would welcome them to the program and let
them blaze away. And then I'd try to talk them around.
And I found it was quite easy to get them to back off. Pretty
soon they'd be qualifying or modifying their stance, or
attempting to mollify me. 'Yes, I'll give you that', they'd
say. I soon realised that many callers were, in truth, simply
rehearsing ideas or restating the opinions that had been
endorsed on other programs. With comparatively few
exceptions it seemed to me that the bluster and bombast
on talk-back radio often camouflaged confusions and that
dialogue was entirely possible.

Hence Adams' First Law of Talk-Back. Vehemence of
expression does not necessarily indicate depth of
conviction.

A wise young man once convinced me that Australians
weren't, finally, all that racist. It was a time like this when
the jungle drums were beating, when John Howard had
launched his 'immigration debate' on a John Laws
program. I'd given a speech at a multicultural seminar in
which I worried about the bigotry that was rising like yeast
in the ovens of opinion—the talk-back shows and the
letters to the editors of Australia's newspapers.

The young man argued that we were not so much
racists as differencists. That we were into differencism. He
argued that Australians are uncomfortable with any sort of
difference, no matter what it was. We were unhappy with
disability, with eccentricity, with intellectualism, with anything or anyone that didn't conform. Race was simply
another dimension, another ingredient, and perhaps not
the most important one.

Tolerance implies no lack of commitment to one's own beliefs. Rather it condemns the oppression or persecution of others.

John F. Kennedy

I've been involved in mass-media campaigns that have had, at least in the short term, a strong impact on prejudices towards Aborigines in particular and immigrants in general. I've seen them work. They've proved to me that apart from the extremes at either end of the Bell curve, public opinion is like a large blob of jelly that wobbles this way or that, depending on the direction of prevailing winds. If actively encouraged, the jelly will wobble to one side. If those views are countered, it will wobble to the other.

Consequently I now veer between optimism and pessimism on the issue of Australian intolerance. Certainly, until recently, I thought that for all our tensions and frictions we were light years ahead of almost anybody else. That we had, at long last, begun to learn how to deal with difference. But the demons never entirely disappear and they must be dealt with on an ongoing basis. Both personally and socially.

The people contributing to this book are highly educated and dazzlingly credentialed specialists who will provide depth and insight in contrast to the uncertain, conflicting views that I've expressed. But for all my uncertainties, I do know this—Australia must achieve tolerance, at least tolerance, if we've a hope of surviving in an increasingly fragmented, fractured world, let alone in a society that will be Balkanised by the new technologies.

As mass media dies, and it's dying very fast indeed, Australia faces the risk of disintegrating into demographic shards. Ethnicity will be but one ingredient in this process; lifestyle choices and belief systems may be far more influential—and divisive.

Many a nation that marched proudly into the MCG for Melbourne's 1956 Olympics will be missing from the opening ceremony at Sydney's in 2000—while dozens of newly minted states will take their place in the rollcall. And in the midst of such international upheaval, in this political and cartographic maelstrom, Australia has to find both a role and a definition.

The world is crowded with nations created this century by colonists or ideologues, forcing together people who mistrust or hate each other. Now they're reverting to tribalisms that demand international recognition and UN membership. Out of ancient arguments in the Middle East, out of recent butcheries in Africa, out of ethnic cleansing in the Balkans, come more flags, more members of the General Assembly, more beaming, waving Olympic delegations. The fact that the flags are dripping with gore doesn't prevent them from being waved triumphantly. Indeed one's pride in a flag seems predicated on its affinity to a wartime bandage. The bloodier the better.

Australia sits oddly in this world of exclusions. Not for us the insistence on the narrowest of definitions. Despite the efforts of our ethnic cleansers, most of us know that a strident emphasis on faith or ethnicity makes little sense. Australia, thank heavens, isn't that sort of nation. Indeed, we're a sort of generalisation. Behold the land of the bitzer.

Around the world there are would-be and putative nations that insist on one theology, one culture. And if you disagree, you're dead. In Australia we try to cobble together a definition, a destiny, based on the very opposite assumption. Beginning with prisoners and soldiers, and moving onto refugees, opportunists, dreamers and adventurers, we've made a society from the flotsam and jetsam of the world. Not that it's been entirely plain sailing as, from time to time, one group of immigrants has objected to the next. Yet we've gone from a monoculture federation to a multicultural aggregation. And so far the death toll has been limited to some 20,000 Aborigines.

Until recently it seemed that Australia was going to show the world that you can build something enduring out of the materials that have washed onto our shores. A nation built from driftwood. Why not? Little multicoloured tiles can be transformed into majestic mosaics. Apparently conflicting shapes can be parts of a coherent jigsaw.

Let us hope that we can wait patiently, even proudly, for that picture to emerge—that we can save it from the Hansonites who pound at the pieces with their fists.

Promoting choice or undermining unions? The changing nature of tolerance at work

BY JOHN BUCHANAN

Australian unions face an uncertain future. It is well known that membership levels are falling. Currently only 31 per cent of employees are union members, down from 51 per cent in 1976.[1] To add to their woes, unions now also face an increasingly hostile legal environment. New labour laws actively promote non-union employment structures and make it increasingly harder for unions to organise members and recruit non-members. Yet despite these developments, support for the idea of unionism remains high. In 1996 just on two-thirds of Australian voters still believed Australia would be worse off if it did not have unions.[2]

What explains this paradox? Do falling membership levels and increasingly hostile labour laws reflect a rising intolerance for collective forms of organisation? Or are they symptomatic of a new tolerance for more diversity in relationships between management and employees at Australian workplaces? Most popular accounts of the decline of unionism assume that it has been caused by a combination of the two, with emphasis increasingly placed on the latter.

The argument goes something like this: unions have had their day; while they may have been necessary in the past, business today needs more flexibility and workers want more choice. Unions, with their commitment to uniform standards, are irrelevant in today's more 'complex' and fast-moving world. New ways of working require more choices. The industrial relations system needs to promote a plurality of approaches to management–employee relations. Systems involving unions are just one option. Others are just as, if not more, appropriate. The declining fortunes of unions are the outcome of this growing tolerance for diversity—rather than increasing intolerance for unions.

Analyses like this have superficial appeal. What can be wrong with choice? Why shouldn't we have more diversity in our industrial relations system? But this line of argument is limited. The most striking limitation arises from its assumptions about the nature of the employment relationship. At the heart of this position is a presumption about the equality of bargaining power between the individual worker and their employer. But this belief is flawed, particularly since historically workers have had to form unions to redress a very real *inequality*. Legal tolerance for such collectivities was slow in coming, and highly circumscribed when eventually achieved. And recent developments in public policy and labour law have again limited unions' capacity to provide an effective counterbalance to the power of management. So, while current reforms are promoted as a means of increasing choice, they have primarily worked to curtail employees' ability to organise effectively (i.e. autonomously) of their employers.

There are four related questions that need to be addressed in light of this:

- Why do unions exist?
- How have they evolved in Australia?
- What's happening to them today?
- Are they still needed?

The challenge for unions today is *not* simply to re-establish levels of tolerance for collective forms of organisation enjoyed in the past. The priority must be to redefine their role and priorities so that they can function effectively at workplace level, as well as at industry and national levels. This will allow them to establish and maintain basic standards, and to play an effective role in taking up issues that are of major concern to their members at the workplace on a day-to-day basis.

Why do unions exist?

In most OECD countries (with the exception of New Zealand) unions enjoy special support and encouragement under the law. The rationale for this situation arises from the long recognised inequality of bargaining power between individual workers and the firms that hire them. The nature of this inequality was noted as early as 1776 in Adam Smith's *The Wealth of Nations*:

A landlord, a farmer, a master manufacturer, or merchant, though they did not employ a single workman, could generally live a year or two upon the stocks which they have already acquired. Many workmen could not subsist a week, few could subsist a month, and scarce any a year without employment. In the long run the workman may be necessary to his master as his master is to him, but the necessity is not so immediate.[3]

Because of this, it is usual for governments to maintain minimum standards (e.g. minimum wage laws) and promote autonomous organisations of employees—unions. Autonomy from management is important because without that independence the ability of employee representatives to negotiate and represent employee interests effectively could be compromised. The importance of this principle of autonomous organisation has been overlooked by many commentators shaping public policy today.[4]

How have unions evolved?

Collective organisations of employees first emerged in Australia in the early nineteenth century. These 'combinations' as they were known, initially took quite a rudimentary form. Their first priorities concerned addressing long hours of work, arduous (and often dangerous) working conditions and low rates of pay.[5] Early achievements such as the eight-hour day and Saturday half-day holiday were often lost during subsequent recessions. Yet the rights of these organisations to operate and exist as collective entities were never recognised by judges in the common law courts.

According to judge-made or 'common' law, unions were
(and indeed remain) nothing more than criminal conspira-
cies established to restrain trade.[6] By definition then, all
unionists were, at common law, criminals.

Fortunately, things began to improve in the latter part
of the nineteenth century. Colonial governments, following
examples from the British Parliament, initially provided
unions with immunities from the more draconian elements
of the common law. After the highly disruptive strikes of
the 1890s in the pastoral, mining and maritime industries,
new laws were introduced to encourage the orderly management of industrial relations. The mechanism used to
achieve this was a system of quasi-judicial tribunals established to conciliate and, if necessary, arbitrate on industrial
disputes. The machinery of conciliation and arbitration
explicitly recognised the role of collective employee and
employer organisation in the maintenance of harmony in
the labour market. Indeed unions were granted a number
of key statutory rights in return for supporting and helping
to enforce award standards. These included rights to
inspect employers' time and wages books, and exclusive
rights to represent employees in particular parts of the
labour market once they were registered in order to mini-
mise demarcation disputes. In few other countries has the
State taken such an active role in industrial relations in
general, and in tolerating and, indeed, supporting unions
specifically.

Between 1920 and the mid 1980s, union membership
oscillated between 45 and 55 per cent of the workforce.[7]
Over this period, unions, through a combination of nego-
tiation, industrial action and use of arbitration, have initiated campaigns that provided the basis for most of the

employment conditions enjoyed by Australian workers today. Key achievements have included:

- a comprehensive system of award-based minimum rates of pay which provide for more than a subsistence standard of living;
- a steady reduction in standard hours of work from around 60–70 hours per week at the turn of the century to 38–40 today;
- annual leave;
- long service leave;
- equal pay for women;
- rights for workers whose employment has been terminated or adversely affected by technological change; and
- superannuation.[8]

Moreover, from 1983 to 1996, the union movement actively participated in the development and implementation of major public policies concerning wages, social security and health. Under the Accord between the ACTU and the Federal Government, unions agreed to restrain overall (or aggregate) wages growth as long as supportive taxation and public expenditure policies were pursued. This strategy involved the more militant segments of the union movement foregoing potentially large wage increases in return for higher levels of employment growth and greater overall gains for lower paid workers and welfare recipients. As a result of this strategy, peak-level union representatives enjoyed unprecedented levels of influence on public policy. The actual outcomes of the Accord strategy still remain the subject of debate. There is no disputing, however, that during its early stages the Accord delivered one of the highest rates of employment growth in the OECD and successfully established a universal health insurance system (i.e. Medicare).

The achievements of the union movement since Federation have been considerable. But while unions have enjoyed a high level of official recognition and influence, especially in recent times, this recognition has come at a price. In return for official tolerance (technically known as recognition), unions were limited, by law, in the types of activities they could undertake. Most importantly, they were expressly prevented from interfering with management activities, which were quaintly known as 'management prerogatives'.[9] With the exception of some notable historical and contemporary examples (e.g. coalmining, the waterfront, large manufacturing and construction sites), Australian unions traditionally have been quite weakly organised at the workplace level. And even though the legal doctrine of the managerial prerogative has gradually declined in recent years, in most Australian workplaces management continues, as a matter of practice, to make most of the important decisions unilaterally.[10]

A number of observers have noted the effects this has had on Australian workplaces. For example, the US academic Milton Derber noted in the early 1970s that Australian employers enjoyed significantly greater freedom in managing their employees than their American counterparts.[11] And Chris Wright, in his recent history of Australian employers, has argued that currently our managers are reasserting control at workplace level by rolling back the limited incursions made on management prerogatives in the 1970s and 1980s on issues such as obligations to consult and the management of working time arrangements.[12]

Despite what many people believed, or assumed, at the height of the ACTU's influence with the Federal Labor Government in the late 1980s and early 1990s, union organisation at most workplaces was generally non-existent or very underdeveloped. For example, the first comprehensive survey of Australian workplace industrial relations conducted in 1990 revealed that the majority of Australian workplaces (57 per cent) did not have any union members. More importantly, even where they did have members, many (around 20 per cent) did not have any local union representatives. And even where there *were* local union representatives, most did little more than recruit members and spend less than one hour per week on union business.[13] Clearly the legal tolerance of unions and their involvement in public policy did not nurture a strong union presence on the job!

This meant that the perceived growing influence of unions in macro policy-making under the Accord with the Labor Government (1983–1996) actually coincided with a weak and declining union influence at workplace level. So the challenge for unions is not just to restore the level of acceptance and support they once enjoyed at industry and national levels, but as well, they must redefine their objectives and gain greater acceptance and recognition at the local and, especially, the workplace level. Yet public policy and labour law is working to make this even more difficult to achieve.

Unions today

Evidence of a declining public policy and legal tolerance for unionism isn't hard to find. Arguably the clearest expression of this sentiment has been the steady restructuring of industrial laws intended to weaken or reduce the protections previously enjoyed by unions. These changes have included reforms directly designed to limit unions' capacity to organise their current members or recruit new ones. Typical have been increases in the fines and sanctions that can be imposed on unions for taking industrial action. The most extensive of these have been increased sanctions for unions taking supportive or solidarity action (so-called secondary boycotts). It's the old move of divide and conquer. Other initiatives have been more subtle but no less effective: the reduction of union officials' right to inspect time and wages books, for example, is a very effective way of reducing a union's ability to maintain award standards. Increasing constraints on union organisers' right of entry to workplaces also makes it difficult to recruit new members.

These limitations on union organising capabilities are not, however, the key features of the declining policy tolerance for unions. Of greater significance are initiatives specifically directed at making unions *irrelevant*. In Australia today this takes two forms: non-union employment agreements and the formation of government agencies established to deal with workers' grievances.

The rise of non-union employment agreements (either individual contracts—often known as Australian Workplace Agreements—or non-union collective agreements) gives managers the capacity to bypass the unions in setting employees' wages and conditions. Individual contracts, by definition, make it difficult for workers to organise collectively. This was Comalco's strategy at its Bauxite and Kaolin mine at Weipa, a case that excited considerable national attention in late 1995.[14] Unions in the coal and maritime industries undertook concerted action in support of employees who were discriminated against because they rejected individual contracts and preferred the union to bargain on their behalf. This strike action resulted in the unionists at Weipa achieving recognition of their capacity to bargain collectively to achieve similar outcomes to those achieved through individual contracts. Sanctions against solidarity action of this nature are now easier to invoke. Collective union resistance to individual contracts will, therefore, be harder to organise in the future. Just as threatening, if not more, are non-union collective agreements. Previously unions had an automatic right to negotiate a collective agreement with an employer where they had any union members present. Now they must win a 'valid majority' of employees consent before they get the right to settle such an agreement. If they fail, the employer can then initiate their own 'collective agreement'.[15] A system similar to this has worked for many years in the United States to limit unions' ability to negotiate agreements for their members in workplaces where management wishes to exclude them.

This system will make unions increasingly irrelevant. A recent example is the Federal Government's new Office of the Employment Advocate. This office deals with grievances of individuals concerned by or dissatisfied with their Australian Workplace Agreement (their individual contract of employment). The handling of individual grievances has traditionally been one of the prime activities of unions. In the early 1990s, 88 per cent of workplace union delegates reported that this was the task they performed most frequently—and they also reported it was the most time-consuming.[16] At a time when the Coalition Government is advocating a reduction in the size of government, it is ironic that it is promoting an extension of the state activity where it works to undermine unions.

Reforms like this have been advanced in the name of increasing choice and 'restoring balance' in the industrial relations system. Unions, it is often claimed in Coalition policy, should not have a privileged legal status but rather should submit 'to the ordinary law of the land'.[17] Are unions still relevant today? And even if they are, should they be entitled to special legal support of the kind they previously enjoyed under our system of conciliation and arbitration?

Are unions still necessary?

Prima facie, many workers appear to believe that they don't need unions. As noted earlier, over the last 20 years union membership levels have fallen by 20 percentage points, and now cover less than one worker in three. Have unions served their purpose? Recent reports on employees' working conditions indicate there is still plenty of work for unions to do.

In 1994 the Federal Department of Industrial Relations surveyed over 10,000 workers to get their views on life at work.[18] The results revealed that 42 per cent of employees surveyed were less satisfied with their employers than they had been a year earlier.[19] A follow-up survey conducted 12 months later revealed growing stress and dissatisfaction with work.[20] When asked how change at the workplace had affected the quality of their lives, over 55 per cent of the workers taking part reported that effort and stress had increased on the job. These findings are summarised below.

Table 1: **Employee views of change at the workplace in the last 12 months, September 1995**

Employee view of change	Percentage of employees		
	Higher	No Change	Lower
Work effort	58	36	4
Stress on the job	50	41	7
Satisfaction with work/family balance	14	58	26
Satisfaction with job	30	40	29

Source: Department of Industrial Relations, Enterprise Bargaining in Australia, 1995 Report, Australian Government Publishing Service, Canberra, 1996

This information builds on earlier findings about the arbitrary way in which change is managed at the workplace. When asked whether consultation concerning major changes affecting the workplace in recent times was adequate, about half (46 per cent) of 19,000 workers surveyed in 1995 reported that they had not had a fair say in the process.[21] This confirms data collected since the late 1980s on the poor consultative practices amongst Australian managers.[22] Many Australian managers, it seems, are incapable of or uninterested in involving employees in key issues affecting their working lives.

This evidence would suggest that if workers could leave their managers as easily as they can leave their unions, we would be talking about the 'crisis in management'. Most workers, of course, do not have such a choice.

In addition to increased stress at work and growing dissatisfaction with management, many workers are also experiencing a deterioration in the quality of their working time arrangements. Some of the key developments in this regard are:

- *hours worked by full-time employees are at their highest level for 30 years* (Between 1966 and 1986 average hours worked by full-time workers ranged between 40.5 and 41.5 per week. In the mid 1990s they are around 42.5 hours. Most of the increase in hours appears to come from rising levels of unpaid overtime.);
- *the number of casuals in the workforce has risen dramatically* (In 1984 only 15.8 per cent of employees were employed on this basis. By 1995 the proportion had risen to 24 per cent.); and
- *the number of part-timers wanting to work more hours is on the rise* (In 1986 only 16.9 per cent of part-timers fell into this category. By 1995, 28.3 per cent wanted to work more hours each week.).[23]

These developments have contradictory implications for unions. On the one hand they make it harder to organise the workforce. Rising levels of precarious and insecure forms of employment make it difficult for unions to contact and recruit members at the workplace. Indeed, these developments go a long way to explaining the decline in union membership. For example, only 14.7 per cent of casuals are union members compared to 41.3 per cent of permanent employees.[24] On the other hand, these developments also provide a potentially powerful impetus for organising disaffected employees, because, to date, management has shown little concern about their future. Employers are generating these outcomes, not through a conspiracy to undermine conditions, but because of pressures to cut costs in the face of commercial competition and pressure from shareholders. Unions, if they are to win back the hearts and minds of employees, need to confront these issues on a multi-employer and potentially nationwide basis. Hours of work and casualisation provided the core around which unions originally established themselves. These core issues still need to be addressed today.

An effective response requires new approaches. Until recently, union strategies were predicted on the assumption of employees working in permanent, full-time jobs. This is no longer valid for growing numbers of workers. Organising strategies at both workplace and community levels will need to change if unions are to successfully meet today's challenges.

Fortunately there is plenty of experience and new ideas to draw on. Writers such as Kathleen Thelen have clarified the issues nicely. She argues that the key challenge is to strike a new balance between activity at both industry and national levels, but with relevance and innovation at the workplace. As she notes:

> Central unions can ill afford to lose their ability to define labo[u]r's overall agenda, but this ability to coordinate and define must be confused with centralised bargaining per se. A central union may choose (or be forced) to pursue

centrally defined goals decentrally ... Organisational
depth (rather than central strength alone) and unions' sub-
national defences will in large measure determine how
labo[u]r weathers the economic strains of the current
period.[25]

New approaches will require the development of new
institutions. A simple restoration of old laws and rights is
not the answer. The challenge is to move beyond the
limited legal 'tolerance' or recognition unions enjoyed in
the past. Instead, a broader notion of rights to take coordinated action is needed on three fronts: at workplace,
industry and national levels. In this way unions can become
more effective and accountable institutions that simultaneously protect and advance employees while helping with
economic development at workplace, industry and national
levels.

Examples of how this can be achieved are provided by
the contrasting experiences of leading North American and
European unions in their response to economic restructuring in the 1980s and 1990s.[26] The essence of these initiatives has been the development of arrangements which
simultaneousely promote the benefits of coordination at
industry and national levels with autonomy at workplace
and enterprise levels. Australia's award system has the
potential to provide an effective framework for promoting
a labour market based on this principal of 'coordinated
flexibility'. The current preoccupation with 'choice',
'decentralisation' and 'deregulation' has meant that the
potential gains that could be achieved by enhancing, not
undermining, our current industrial relations structures
have been overlooked by both sides of politics. As the limits

of the current approach to 'reform' become more apparent, in the future greater attention should be given to enhancing, not undermining, collective institutions such as unions and awards.

Conclusion

There can be no doubt that relations between managers, employees and unions are undergoing a profound re-alignment in Australia today. Union membership is falling. Non-union agreements, promoted by law, are set to increase. Functions previously regarded as quintessentially union activities, such as handling individual grievances, are now potentially to be handled by the State. Some commentators see this as the beginning of a new era of choice— a new age of tolerance for diversity in the industrial relations system as the rigidities of the old collectivist system are removed.

Such a reading of the current situation is wrong. The inequality of bargaining power at the heart of the employment relationship remains as real today as it was a hundred years ago. Special legal tolerance was extended to unions then, to partially redress that inequality. The development of special legal principles to regulate particular types of social relations is not unique to industrial relations—many areas of life are governed by distinctive, non–common law, legal doctrines. And this applies to the commercial world as much as to the world of work. The tolerance originally extended to unions came at a price: limited ability to influence activity on the shop floor. The challenge is to rethink what tolerance for collective organisations of employees means if the inequalities in bargaining power are to be effectively redressed. If new rights of 'tolerance' or recognition are to be effective, they will have to be based on organisational structures firmly anchored in the workplace acting in coordinated fashion to address the key issue of working time, work intensification and growing labour market insecurity.

Problems of this nature cannot be addressed by re-establishing the old regime, the one that prevailed before the most recent wave of reforms began. Instead it will require coming up with a new approach to the rights and obligations surrounding managers, employees and unions in ways that enhance both efficiency, equity and account-ability. The elements of a new approach mean that public policy must move beyond its current preoccupations with decentralisation and deregulation. Encouraging developments in the literature point to the potential of working on the notion of 'coordinated flexibility' as focus for reform that move beyond the limitations of the old regulatory regime and the weaknesses associated with the 'free market' inspired reforms of today.

Notes

1 Australian Bureau of Statistics, *Trade Union Members*, Australia, August 1976, 1996 Cat. No. 6325.0.

2 ACIRRT/Newspoll, *Attitudes to Unions and Work*; Poll conducted in April 1996.

3 Adam Smith, *The Wealth of Nations*, Modern Library, New York, 1937, p. 66.

4 The only notable exceptions to this amongst economics commentators are Ken Davidson at the *Age* and Ross Gittins at the *Sydney Morning Herald*.

5 A good summary of the extensive literature on early Australian unions is provided by Greg Patmore, *Australian Labour History*, Longman Cheshire, Melbourne, 1991, especially Chapter 3.

6 D. Smith and D. Rawson, *Trade Union Law in Australia: The Legal Status of Australian Trade Unions*, Butterworths, Sydney, 1985.

7 Raymond Markey, *In Case of Oppression: The Life and Times of the Labor Council of New South Wales*, Pluto Press, Sydney, 1994, pp. 565–66.

8 A useful summary of the history behind these standard conditions of employment is provided by Bede Healey, *Federal Arbitration in Australia: An Historical Outline*, Georgian House, Melbourne, 1972.

9 It should be noted that this was not unique to Australia. See for example Keith Sisson, 'Employers and the Structure of Collective Bargaining' in S. Tolliday and J. Zeitlin (eds), *The Power to Manage?*, Routledge, London, 1991, pp. 256–71, for an overview of similar developments in most other OECD countries.

10 A very comprehensive account of this aspect of Australian workplaces is provided in Christopher Wright, *The Management of Labour: A History of Australian Employers*, Oxford University Press, Melbourne, 1995.

11 M. Derber, 'Labor–Management Relations in the Metalworking Industries of Three Countries', *Journal of Industrial Relations*, 13(1), pp. 1–23.

12 Christopher Wright, op. cit., Chapter 7.

13 R. Callus, A. Moorehead, M. Cully and J. Buchanan, *Industrial Relations at Work: The Australian Workplace Industrial Relations Survey*, Australian Government Publishing Service, Canberra, 1991, Chapter 5.

14 For union and management accounts of this matter, see respectively P. Gorman, *Weipa: Where Australian Unions Drew their 'Line in the Sand' with CRA*, Weipa Industrial Committee/Construction, Forestry, Mining and Energy Union, Sydney, 1996, and J. T. Ludecke, *The Line in the Sand: The Long Road to Staff Employment at Comalco*, Wilkinson Books, Melbourne, 1996.

15 See for example S170LE of the Workplace Relations and Other Legislation Amendment Bill 1996.

16 R. Callus et al, op. cit., p. 109.

17 John Hewson and Tim Fischer, *Fightback! It's your Australia*, Canberra, 1991.

18 Federal Department of Industrial Relations, *Enterprise Bargaining in Australia: 1994 Report*, Australian Government Publishing Service, Canberra, 1995.

19 ibid, p. 379.

20 Federal Department of Industrial Relations, *Enterprising Bargaining in Australia: 1995 Report*, Australian Government Publishing Service, Canberra, 1996.

21 ibid, p. 86.

22 R. Callus et al, op. cit., Chapter 9, and M. Short, J. Romeyn and R. Callus, *Reform and Bargaining at the Workplace and the Enterprise: Evidence from Two Surveys*, Australian Government Publishing Service, Canberra, 1994.

23 The following material is drawn from John Buchanan and Sue Bearfield, *Reforming Working Time: Alternatives to Unemployment, Casualisation and Excessive Hours of Work*, Brotherhood of St Laurence, Melbourne, 1997, especially p. 67.

24 Australian Bureau of Statistics, *Trade Union Members*, Australia, August 1994, Product Number 6325.0.40.001.

25 Kathleen Thelen, 'The Politics of Flexibility in the German Metalworking Industries' in Miriam Golden and Jonas Pontusson, *Bargaining for Change: Union Politics in North America and Europe*, Cornell University Press, Ithaca, 1992, p. 243.

26 A summary of these developments is provided in John Buchanan, 'Industrial relations, enterprise bargaining and the continuing relevance of socialist principles' in Tim Battin and Graham Maddox (eds), *Socialism in Contemporary Australia*, Longman, Melbourne, 1996, pp. 135–141.

'An opportunity to change the culture'

BY MARY KALANTZIS AND BILL COPE

On 2 March 1996, the Australian people changed their Federal Government for only the fifth time in half a century. Such changes should be, therefore, truly defining moments. But this particular moment was, at least at first, eerily inarticulate.

On the basics of the Labor Government's agenda, the Coalition seemed to disagree barely at all. There was, for example, no fundamental disagreement with 'big picture issues' such as Mabo and indigenous reconciliation; immigration levels would remain the same; bipartisan support for multiculturalism would continue; and relations with Asia would grow stronger. With little to differentiate the parties, swinging voters could, seemingly reasonably, opt for a change for not much more than change's sake.

In its first six months, the Howard Government was preoccupied with the job of balancing the books after the so-called 'Beazley Black Hole' showed up. The massive cuts in public spending that followed appeared to be an exercise in fiscal rectitude. There was now almost no mention of any of the 'big picture' issues. When it came to defining the nation, projecting a vision of Australia in the world, and imagining our identity, the Howard Government had little to say. Extending the picture metaphor, one cartoonist called Howard a political miniaturist. As hard as it is supposed to be for politicians to inflict fiscal pain, it certainly does not require high-level vision. Indeed, when it's only a matter of subtraction, rejigging the books doesn't take much imagination at all.

Interpreting the opening moments of the Howard years in Australian history is difficult. There are two possible lines of interpretation. Either the 'big picture' issues have been displaced by fiscal miniaturism. Or—to borrow the terminology of Treasurer Peter Costello's main contribution to public discourse in Australia—although there is no 'headline' vision, there is an 'underlying' vision.

Does the beginning of the Howard era represent a significant cultural shift? And if it does, what is it and what will this cultural shift mean for this country? None of these questions can be easily answered. One key may be found in the way Howard continually contrasts his government's vision with the ideological orthodoxies that defined the Keating Government. Rarely, however, are these orthodoxies defined, although that slippery concept 'political correctness' has been frequently employed; but multiculturalism is surely one of them. As is a particular version of Aboriginal Affairs. As is the Republican view of our relationship with England. As is, in fact, a whole way of understanding our history and who we are as Australians.

No longer, Howard asserts, will the Government be dictated to by minority groups or political correctness.

And, along with the rest of the Howard moment in Australian history, there is an 'underlying' subtext as well as the 'headline' text.

* * *

Without a majority in the Senate, the Howard Government had to confront the possibility of having some significant parts of its program blocked. Howard reflected on why he wanted his program passed in an August 1996 interview with *Business Review Weekly*:

> You've got an opportunity to change the culture, you've got an opportunity for there to be a flow-through benefit and you've got an opportunity for the Government to really take root in the community.[1]

So politics for Howard actually is, it would seem, a lot more that an accounting exercise—a job of balancing the books. There is also the cultural project—one which may need time to take root in the community. For Howard also wants to take his 'opportunity to change the culture'. As he reminded a gathering of Liberal Party faithful in Sydney, 'government is not only about dollars and cents and economic goals and economic objectives but government is also about values, and government is also about the way we think about ourselves'.[2]

When he became Prime Minister, Howard said:

> One of the goals I set myself, was quite simply to bring about a restoration where people felt a little more freely, if the mood struck them, to talk about controversial issues without fear of being branded as a racist or some other

kind of bigot for daring to bring up those subjects. I think
one of the many criticisms I had of the former Government was the way in which it used a form of social
censorship to intimidate people out of debating difficult,
sensitive and controversial issues. I think we had become
almost too politically correct to a fault before the second
of March.[3]

The 'headline' text of Howard's argument was, in this
way, about free speech and open debate. Regarding political correctness he could say that 'some simply call it
intimidatory attitudes to free speech'.[4] The 'underlying'
subtext was an attack on interest groups—the so-called
multicultural 'industry', the Aboriginal 'industry', the arts
'industry', the public broadcasting 'industry' and the list
goes on—to which Labor was alleged to defer at the
expense of the 'battlers' and the small business people of
'mainstream Australia'.

Howard's the 'Australia I Believe In' statement of 1995
also argued that 'the divisions within our society have been
accentuated over recent years and that the political strategy
of the Keating Government has been part of the cause'.
The Coalition was, therefore, committed to 'ending the
increasing divisiveness in our society'. It would defend the
mainstream against the special interest groups because 'the
losers have been the men and women of mainstream
Australia whose political voice is too often muffled and
ignored'.[5]

Who *is* this 'mainstream Australia'? The answer to this
seems to be everybody other than the 'minority special
interest groups'. And the cultural profile of this Australia
was clear. It was middle Australia, white Australia, settled

rather than recently immigrant Australia. Its essence was quintessentially to be found in the mateship of the bush.

> I think one of the things that tugs at the heartstrings of Australians ... when we think of the decline of the economic strengths and the depopulation of rural areas of Australia, we think we are losing something which has been indelibly Australian for as long as we have thought of ourselves as Australians and that is the sense of community and mateship and looking after each other in adversity, which you find in rural Australia.[6]

If there is to be a cultural transformation, it is towards this ideal. It is to reduce the divisive influence of minority interest groups and increase national cohesion. 'I'm a one nation man', said Mr Howard. And in our relationships in the Asian region, we are clearly not an 'Asian' nation. Our historical and cultural affinities, as well as our military alliances, are to be with the United States and Britain.

Here the Prime Minister can be seen to be taking a clear stand on one of the central tensions in twentieth-century Australian political history. In its more clear-sighted and articulate moments, the Keating version of inclusiveness recognised and built upon differences in history and experience. Multiculturalism was a way of making people feel a part of Australia by recognising and valuing immigrant differences. Native Title and Aboriginal Reconciliation were ways of making indigenous peoples part of Australia by recognising their distinctive historical experience. And an outward-looking economic vision embraced our increasingly important trade and immigrant connections into the Asian region. These then are also the critical elements of the divisiveness which Howard sees as inimical to the interests of mainstream Australia.

Howard's 'one nation' version of inclusiveness takes another historical tack, reminiscent of that other great moment of 'mateship'—Federation. In establishing the 'mateship' of the nation—one homogenous Australia with cultural and constitutional ties back to England—diversity was then also seen to be a threat. Aborigines were 'protected' on reserves until such time as they could reach the level of civilisation that had been achieved by the 'mates'. The borders were sealed against those who, by virtue of racial and cultural inferiority, could never really be our 'mates'. Hence the White Australia Policy; the deportation of Kanakas; and the desultory business of Empire Settlement, the inter-war scheme bringing migrants from the British Isles to Australia. And our industry and local markets were 'protected' by high tariff barriers, with a special eye to the regional threat of Asia. In more recent incarnations, the 'one nation' version of our history and politics allowed more latitude to different 'interest groups'—it allowed differences in the interim on condition that assimilation would occur in the medium term; it allowed that we might trade with the region, but not at the expense of our identity.

Neither of these two approaches to inclusiveness—the more outward-looking, pluralist approach based on the recognition of diversity and regional location and the more inward-looking, 'one nation' approach attempting to create national uniformity—has been the monopoly of Labor or the Conservatives. It was the Fraser Coalition Government which first introduced multiculturalism and Aboriginal self-management. In contrast, from the late nineteenth century there has been a pervasive protectionist strand in the Labor tradition, ever suspicious of the consequences of open labour markets, which has defended the racial and national unity of the working 'mates'.

So, in the great rip-tide of competing visions of the Australian nation, it seems we may have switched courses in 1996 in a very profound way. We are changing the basis of the political order. The language of pluralism is to be replaced by a revived language of a singular and unitary nation. One conventional wisdom replaces another.

Yet questions remain. Will it work? Is the retreat from pluralism possible or even economically sensible? At best, the problem with Howard's 'one nation' and mateship nostalgia is that it might be too late in the era of local diversity and relentless globalisation. At worst it might be counter-productive nonsense. But to understand the genesis of the Howard vision—his underlying cultural subtext—we need first to examine the roots of conservative political failure in the 1980s and 1990s.

*   *   *

In 1988, during his first stint as Opposition Leader, Mr Howard had stood out publicly against the level of Asian immigration. 'I think there are some in the community who are concerned that the pace of change has been too great,' he said. He recognised the issue was a sensitive one, adding the convenient rider that, personally, he did not think there were too many Asians in Australia. Nevertheless, he went on, 'any political leader has to take account of the capacity of society to absorb change. To do so is not to be racist but to be realistic. Votes have nothing to do with it.' He also said that 'although the original intent of multiculturalism may have been desirable, it has gone off the rails'. Joining the affray soon after was Senate National Party Leader John Stone, but with somewhat less circumspection. Most Australians, he said baldly, were 'totally angry about the way the present mix of the immigration program appeared to bear no relationship to the existing structure of the population'.[7]

Howard was meanwhile reorienting the Coalition parties' stance on immigration in the direction of what he called a 'One Australia' policy. This was full of assurances that it would not be discriminatory, but had a ring that nevertheless sounded a bit like 'White Australia'. The intention certainly seemed to be that one of the objectives of immigration policy was to ensure national homogeneity.

At the time the newly elected New South Wales Liberal Premier, Nick Greiner, publicly disagreed with Howard and Stone. 'We have a multicultural society, we will continue to have a multicultural society in our life-times—there's almost no decision that anyone can make to change that.'[8] And former Liberal Prime Minister Malcolm Fraser, addressing the Federation of Ethnic Communities Councils Congress, indirectly also rebuked Howard. He spoke of the virtues of diversity and the inevitable changes in composition of the immigration intake.[9] So when the issue was finally debated in Parliament, a number of senior Liberals, including two former immigration ministers, crossed the floor and voted with the Labor Government. One of those who crossed over was Philip Ruddock, who was to be given the portfolio of Immigration and Multicultural Affairs in March 1996.

Howard lost his job shortly after his Asian immigration statements in a swift and unexpected palace coup, later admitting that his position in the immigration debate had been a major factor contributing to his downfall. As a lead-up to his reinstatement as Opposition leader in 1995, there-fore, he expressed his regrets about these 1988 statements. He had been mistaken, he said, but now his views had changed.

After his first disastrous stint as Opposition Leader, Howard had been replaced by his old party foe, Andrew Peacock, but once again the Liberals stumbled on the 'race' issue. This time it was in relation to the Multi Function Polis—a high-tech city of the future to be built by Japanese investors in Australia. As Opposition Leader, Peacock said, he objected to the establishment of an enclave of foreigners in Australia. 'Peacock Stirs Asian Debate', shouted the newspaper headlines.[10] So when Peacock lost the next elec-tion, his handling of the Multi Function Polis issue was allotted a large part of the blame.

Slow learners, seemingly, for yet again in the 1992–93 election campaign, the Coalition stumbled on immigration, racism and diversity. This time the Opposition parties were led by John Hewson, who, like Howard before him, expressed his scepticism about multiculturalism and sug-gested that immigration levels were too high. In most accounts of the subsequent March 1993 election, the pro-posed Goods and Services Tax has been singled out as Hewson's 'Achilles heel'. Hewson's tax was informed by hard economic rationalism and a resolve to balance the budget at any cost. There would be massive cutbacks to the ABC, the public service, the arts, and so on—and immi-gration would also be cut.

The Hewson agenda represented for the first time an elevation of the numbers game of economic management as the main game of politics. But perhaps most importantly, it meant that issues of multiculturalism, Aboriginal reconciliation, Australia's sense of nationhood and our relationship with the Asian region were displaced. Meanwhile, although it was badly reported in the media, Labor played a cultural tune to women; to ethnic groups, with the assurance of multiculturalism; to Aborigines; to those who believe our future lies in our connections with Asia and not to England; to arts groups; and to community organisations. These were the groups that helped secure Paul Keating his election victory that year. Labor played to precisely the interest group politics that Howard as Prime Minister was later to find so reprehensible. And, against the economic odds, Labor won.

Here are some revealing snapshots of a barely told political story. Sydney's third largest newspaper, after the *Herald* and the *Telegraph-Mirror*, is the *Australian Chinese Daily*, with a quite remarkable circulation of 15,000. Raymond Teng, chief editor, said that his paper ran lots of stories on multiculturalism in the lead-up to the 1993 election and that one of the critical problems for the Opposition was that it did not explain itself clearly. There was fear about what they would do to immigrant communities if they gained power. This is supported by Patrick Poon, of the Sydney-based, Chinese-language newspaper, *Sing Tao Daily*, who conducted a pre-election survey in Sydney, Melbourne and Brisbane which showed over 50 per cent of Chinese Australians were inclined to vote for Labor, because they felt more secure with them. In order of importance, the issues they highlighted were migration, Medicare and taxation. John Hewson, like John Howard before him, created anxiety because he was critical of multiculturalism. The major failure of the Coalition, said Poon, was that it failed to explain itself to immigrant communities. As business people, and given the historical experience of Indo-China, Australia's Chinese immigrants are by no means a natural Labor constituency. Yet theirs was not an isolated fear. Anwar Harib, editor of the Arabic-language *El Telegraph*, believed that immigrant communities at that time were bitter about the way immigration issues were handled by the Opposition. 'If we are 30 per cent of the population, then 30 per cent of the issues should relate to us,' he said. 'The Labor Party was obviously closer and warmer to migrants.'[11]

By March 1993 then, there had been three consecutive elections which the Coalition had lost, at least in part, for its mishandling of issues of immigration, culture and diversity. Even slow learners eventually get the message. After three elections marred by these stumbles, the 1996 election was going to be different.

* * *

Journalists who followed the 1996 campaign closely say that Howard's speech to launch the Coalition's Immigration and Multiculturalism and Settlement Policies before ethnic communities at the Heidelberg Town Hall on 9 February 1996, was his best. The audience was a carefully selected mix of party faithful, ethnic community leaders and the ethnic press, and the impression they took away was very favourable. Howard spoke warmly, positively and without notes.

The press release, sent out that night, said that 'the Leader of the Opposition, Mr John Howard, strongly affirmed the Coalition's continuing commitment to a multicultural Australia in which all Australians are able to participate fully in our inclusive society'. And the opening words of the Multicultural Affairs and Settlement Policy launched that night promised that 'The Coalition is committed to maintaining and further enhancing Australia's unique and enriching cultural diversity'.[12] Not only were they finally getting the rhetoric right, but there were tangible promises of increases in funding for adult English teaching ($17 million); community organisations ($20 million); and new funding for an anti-racism education program ($10 million). There was even a promise that the immigration intake would remain at least at its current levels. And when sceptics quizzed Shadow Immigration Minister Jim Short on whether some of the key Labor initiatives such as the Office of Multicultural Affairs in the Department of the Prime Minister and Cabinet would stay, his answer was a categorical 'yes'.

Unlike the 1993 election, therefore, the ethnic press reported the event and the Coalition's policy in a positive light. And, unlike 1993 when the Liberal Party had not advertised in the ethnic press because Party Secretary Andrew Robb thought it was a waste of money, in 1996 the ethnic press was blitzed in the last week of the election campaign with a massive advertising campaign stressing the Coalition's commitment to immigration and multiculturalism. Some of the gloss was, unfortunately, taken off the Coalition's stance by Peter Costello's 'Meeting our Commitments' document which proposed that new migrants' waiting period for eligibility to social security benefits be extended from six months to two years. But not too much of the gloss. After all, the very idea of a waiting period as a budget reduction measure had been invented by the

Labor Party under Immigration Minister Gerry Hand.

In his post-election analysis of the results, Andrew Robb explained the importance of opinion polling in the lead-up to March 1996. Rather than present the community with a comprehensive, if somewhat threatening, economic ideology as they had in 1993, the Coalition did what the polls told it to do—move to the centre. Hence, when it came to immigration and multiculturalism, not only had Howard recanted his 1988 position, he was seen by television cameras and newspaper reporters eating Chinese meals with Asian community leaders and meeting with Greek Orthodox priests.

The election results later showed that the strategy had worked, for the Liberal Party's exit polling on election day showed a 6 per cent swing amongst ethnic communities. Whereas the Coalition's Catholic vote had trailed Labor's by nine points in 1993, when Hewson's severe economic rationalism was criticised by the Catholic Social Welfare Commission and other Catholic leaders, it was ahead of Labor by 10 points in 1996.[13]

Perhaps the most significant defining feature of the campaign were the racist statements of several renegade candidates. On Australia Day, far-north Queensland National Party candidate, Bob Burgess, called the citizenship ceremonies held around Australia that day 'de-wogging ceremonies'. Soon after, National Party colleague and sitting member for Kennedy, Bob Katter, slipped not only in criticising 'femo-Nazis' and 'eco-Nazis', but 'slanty-eyed ideologues' as well. National Party leader Tim Fischer immediately reprimanded these men for their indiscretions. Then Liberal Party candidate for the southern Queensland seat of Oxley, Pauline Hanson, complained about the special treatment Aborigines received at the expense of 'the whites'. She was disendorsed by the Queensland Liberals without Mr Howard being asked. This decision was no doubt made easier by the fact that Oxley, the former seat of Labor leader and Governor-General Bill Hayden, was safe Labor territory and the Liberal Party held out little prospect of winning it.

These racist comments became the most reported single issue of the whole election campaign, with a total of 2603 media mentions. All in all, however, they did the Coalition no harm for the Coalition's response was swift. Victorian Liberal Premier Jeff Kennett said on 15 February, 'Bob Katter and his colleagues have to be mugs of the first order. I don't know how people like that can honestly stand for political office claiming to represent all their community equally.' As penance, perhaps, the National Party thought it necessary to advertise its support for immigration and multiculturalism in the ethnic press, despite the ethnic media's predominantly city base and city circulation.

Nor did renegade Coalition candidates have a monopoly on racism. There was also the renegade Labor candidate for Kalgoorlie, Graeme Campbell, standing as an independent on an anti-immigration, anti-multiculturalism platform.

Yet in all four seats, the electoral results favoured these candidates. Katter was returned with a significantly increased majority; Burgess lost to a Liberal candidate, but registered an improvement in the National Party vote; while Campbell and Hanson won as independents. These results might be seen as a victory of racism and a defeat for tolerance.

However, the story is actually much more complicated than this. Bob Katter, for instance, is of Lebanese extraction. When asked, he says 'I'm an Australian, and you know who I am'. Which, given the extraordinary, if frequently unrecognised, history and contemporary experience of diversity in north Queensland, everyone does. He is highly respected in Aboriginal communities, having granted freehold title to many of them as a former state Minister for Aboriginal Affairs, which is why he won 10 of the 12 booths in Mount Isa—a predominantly immigrant and Aboriginal town. Nor can Graeme Campbell simply be labelled as an unreconstructed racist, for he won very strong support in the Aboriginal communities of northwest Australia. And Hanson's win was one repeated around Australia, in traditional working-class electorates buffeted by industry restructuring and urban decline.

Seemingly to their credit, Mr Howard and Mr Fischer had taken pains to distance themselves from these public statements of the renegade candidates. Interpreting the election results more broadly, there was little joy for racism or bigotry. The Coalition won by taking an essentially bipartisan stand on the 'big picture' issues. Both Mr Howard and Mr Fischer repeatedly stated that their government would be inclusive; that they would govern in the interests of all Australians. This was the reasonable, positive interpretation which could be put on the Coalition's election slogan, 'For All of Us'. On the Republic, Mr Howard had said that although he was himself a monarchist, he was prepared to be persuaded by the people's will and promised to hold a People's Convention. On Mabo, Mr Howard again went to great pains to reassure Australians that he stood behind the principles of Native Title established in the Mabo case and subsequent legislation, particularly after Western Australian Premier Court stated his fundamental opposition to this legislation. What's more, Australia's relationship with Asia even got its own 'Headland' speech from Mr Howard in 1995.

On other big picture items, such as a commitment to a 'fair go' and a 'social safety net', Mr Howard repeatedly assured the Australian people that the Coalition would not dismantle what was already in place. They would do no more than offer 'choice'—a choice that included Medicare and unionism. On the environment, they were at pains to match Labor Party promises. In fact, on all the aspects of the big picture, the Coalition assured Australians that they too shared a sense of the breadth of the canvas. Australians, they insisted, could vote for them and not risk any aspects of the big picture. And vote for them they did.

It is possible moreover that, notwithstanding the Hansons, the Burgesses, the Katters and the Campbells, many Australians believed in the big picture and felt cheated by Labor insofar as it had not delivered on the substance. How else does one explain the fact that those so-called minorities, accused of being the beneficiaries of the big-picture and special-interest-group agendas at the expense of ordinary middle Australia, also voted for the Liberal and National parties? In 1996 larger proportions of ethnic and indigenous communities voted for the Coalition than ever before.

Just as the Coalition parties were finally 'getting it right', the 1996 election represented a moment of cultural failure for the Labor Party. A gap was appearing between Keating's fine big-picture imagery about the benefits of being near Asia and democratic pluralism on the one hand, and on the other, people's experience of its truth on the ground. This applied not only to the experience of 'middle

Australia' but also to the so-called 'minority' groups who shifted their vote so markedly.

While Labor kept a core of voters in ethnic communities, it nevertheless lost ground. This was not just because the Liberal Party wooed ethnic communities with a tenacity not witnessed since the Fraser years, but because members of ethnic communities also felt betrayed by Labor. Tremendous damage was done in the Batman preselection fiasco which forced Martin Ferguson onto a community that wanted to select as a candidate a woman from an ethnic background. It is noteworthy that the only seat in which Labor enjoyed a positive swing was the Melbourne seat held by Andrew Theophanous, Parliamentary Secretary to the Prime Minister on Multicultural Affairs.

Indeed, the whole restructuring agenda led by Martin Ferguson's mates, Ministers Crean and Free, underscored the sense of abandonment felt by immigrant workers. The National Training Reform agenda had already meant that many workers were losing jobs in which they had performed perfectly well for years because they failed written competency tests. There was also uncertainty about Labor's affiliation with the elite rump of a declining union movement which had once again displayed its traditional anxiety about immigration. And Labor's attempt to woo the green vote meant that they were aligned with elements that are frequently anti-immigration and anti-multicultural. Labor's actions belied Labor's words.

Similar things can be said about Mabo and indigenous reconciliation. Keating's Redfern speech remains the most significant statement by any Australian politician about the predicament of Australia's indigenous peoples—what needs to be recognised and what needs to be accomplished. But to many it remained just that—a good speech. All over the country too many indigenous communities, including those who handed Katter and Campbell their votes, felt that Mabo had not delivered on the ground.

Keating's big picture future was also linked to a refiguring of Australian identity and symbols. Here he had a grand and timely vision. With the centenary of Federation and the Sydney Olympics on the horizon, there was an opportunity to match Australia's new conditions with its symbols. But here again, discussion about the Republic continued to be limited to a small, elite group. There was no systematic attempt to integrate the broader community in discussion about the shape and breadth of the changes possible. Mr Keating and his Government thus demonstrated little faith in a people who, the polls said, were increasingly predisposed to the idea. Howard's convention proposal on the other hand was aimed at handing the discussion back to the people.

In this way, it wasn't that the Keating Government failed because it was too focused on narrow interest groups but because it neglected interest groups, particularly at the grassroots community level.

* * *

In an interview just before the election, Mr Howard explained that his vision for the future of Australia was that he wanted Australians to be 'relaxed and comfortable' not just in the present, but about the past as well.[14] Indeed, he wanted us to feel as relaxed and comfortable about ourselves and our history as we had during the halcyon Menzies years.

To be 'relaxed and comfortable' as a serious political agenda has one particular implication when attached to our past—that we shouldn't have to worry too much about the kind of accusations about historical injustice and racism that prompt pluralism as a political approach to inclusiveness. Yet it is a tempting prospect in an age of anxiety, as now.

So the Federal Coalition played it safe and resoundingly won the 1996 election. And with the particular make-up of the election result, it was no longer necessary to assure people that the 'big picture' was much the same as Labor's. Indeed, the rhetoric changed to contrast the Coalition's cultural mission with that of the former government. For mainstream Australia now meant something different, and the electorates who voted in Katter and Hanson and Campbell were surely one aspect of this mainstream.

Immigration and multiculturalism were areas in which this distinction was being made very clearly. When the 1996–97 migration program was announced in July 1996, Immigration and Multicultural Affairs Minister Ruddock was assuring people that the changes did not represent a cut. The Coalition's election promise had, he claimed, been honoured and the planned overall figure for 1996–97 was the same as the average for the past four years. This, of course, was a statistical trick, given that the actual figure did represent a 10 per cent cut on 1995–96, but a plausible one nevertheless.

Mr Howard, on the other hand, was keen to send out a totally different message to that of Ruddock. There was definitely a cut, he told John Laws and his radio listeners, because there had to be. In doing this, the Prime Minister was willing to make it clear that he was breaking his Government's election promise that immigration levels would remain the same. He could have chosen to reassure people, as Mr Ruddock would have counselled, that the policy was not being broken, but he chose not to.

Victoria's Liberal Premier, Jeff Kennett, speedily criticised the decision. Australia needed to grow as a nation, he said. 'Migration has enriched Australia, both economically and culturally.' The reduction in family reunion was 'unfortunate and unnecessary' and the cut in immigration 'would open the floodgates to unwarranted racial comment'. The cuts would send the wrong message to the region, giving Australia an image problem overseas. Although Mr Ruddock had been trying very hard not to send out what Mr Kennett would call the 'wrong message', the Prime Minister had gone out of his way to defeat the best intentions of his Immigration Minister.

Then came the cuts. Fiscal rectitude or anti the multicultural and Aboriginal 'industries'? That is the key question. The $5 million Office of Multicultural Affairs in the Department of Prime Minister and Cabinet was abolished and its functions removed, without funding, to the Immigration Department. The $6 million Bureau of Immigration, Multicultural and Population Research was abolished, with only its statistical function being retained. 'The Bureau has become a casualty as a result partly because of its close association with aggressive immigration and multicultural advocacy within the Keating Government,' said Paul Sheehan in the *Sydney Morning Herald*.[15] In other words, because of its political correctness. The tenor of the Coalition's election platform had been ongoing constructive support for immigration and multiculturalism but nobody could be under any illusion now—neither the ethnic communities nor the anti-immigration lobby—that the reality of government was to be entirely different. Nor could Aboriginal communities be under any illusion when $400 million was cut from the budget of the Aboriginal and Torres Strait Islander Commission, and the Commission was told categorically where the cuts were to be made—in community initiatives rather than mainstream services such as health.

Thriving on controversy, the media also made it its business to attack, ostensibly on behalf of a neglected mainstream Australia, the various lobbies and interest group 'industries'. This is what Mr Howard was referring to when he said the Government was not going to be dictated to by minorities. Against the protests of those he labelled 'the politically correct', former Senator John Stone defended Deputy Prime Minister Tim Fischer's reference to 'the immigration industry' and Howard's reference to 'the Aboriginal industry'.[16] Writing in the *Sydney Morning Herald*, Paul Sheehan claimed that 'Multiculturalism has become a tax-fed industry of lawyers, bureaucrats, politicians and ethnic axe-grinders'. For instance, 'the State-funded anti-utopia at SBS is a metaphor for the evolving fantasy that Australia should be a cultural federation of glorious diversity'. And writing about the New South Wales Anti-Discrimination Board, whose President is former Liberal Senator Chris Puplick (the 'unofficial Godfather of Grievance in New South Wales'), Sheehan declared that 'one of the reasons for high unemployment in New South Wales is the plethora of Thought Police employed by the State. Employers know they can face an inquisition if a job recipient does not work out.'[17]

In an article in the *Financial Review*, Max Walsh calculated that $143 million in 1994–95 went to 1300 community groups—environmental, migrant, women's, welfare, Aboriginal—all pork-barrelling on the part of Labor, and perpetrators of politically correct propaganda. And who can he use to argue this better than former Finance Minister Peter Walsh, who claims that this is how the March 1996 election was really won and lost?

> Today's politically correct vanguard wants to invoke the State's coercive power to impose its uniformity . . . . The press, especially in the Canberra Gallery and the ABC, mortified that the people should swing to candidates who say things which they disapprove, writes them off as regional rednecks unrepresentative of the real Australia. It might ruminate on the fact that the ALP now has a minority of federal politicians in every state and only seven out of 51 House seats in Queensland, WA and SA. No doubt many factors contributed to that disaster, but a geographically widespread rejection of authoritarian PC was one of them.[18]

Communications Minister Senator Alston took up the ABC theme in a radio interview on the 'AM' program. The ABC, he warned, should stop reporting on politically correct stuff, such as Aborigines and multiculturalism, and get back to hard facts, such as the Beazley black hole.

In Aboriginal Affairs, the beginnings of the new vision for Australia included the suggestion that the 1950s policy of assimilation may not have been such a bad idea after all. On 17 June 1996, Aboriginal Affairs Minister Herron launched a book by Geoffrey Partington which argued that

Australia would do well to return to Hasluck's policy of the 1950s.[19] Mr Howard attended the launch, saying that he had heard it was 'a good book'. Dismissing criticism of Herron's statement that we should be reconsidering assimilation, he claimed that his minister had been a victim of the 'thought police'. Throwing his own views into the discussion, Howard said, 'Any notion of self-determination which includes the idea of a nation within a nation is something to which I am totally opposed'. As nobody was really suggesting that we have nations within nations, this has to be interpreted as another way of saying that the Howard government will be pulling back from bipartisan support for cultural pluralism.

All these incidents represent snapshots of what 'changing the culture' means in practice. Howard says it should be possible to attack these groups and their agendas without being branded a racist, but the budget cuts are doing that job, without saying as much.

* * *

There are politics to words, politics to ideas and politics to culture. We always have to be talking about what we are saying. We always have to be thinking why we are thinking and what we are thinking for. And culture will always be politics, as we ponder massive cultural shifts and argue with the agents of cultural change as well as the defenders of various pasts.

Chris Puplick accounts for the current shift in terms of 'the emergence into the Australian political debate of the heretofore marginalised and ignored—women, indigenous Australians, gays and lesbians, the poor, people with disabilities, non-native English speakers, those concerned with economic agendas which are not about economic growth, making money, distributing wealth or rearranging the deckchairs on the financial Titanic. Their emergence is a potential threat to those who ... have done very nicely, thank you, out of the status quo of exclusionism.'[20] For Puplick, the shift represents a retreat from tolerance. 'The recent attacks on what somewhat nebulously has been called "political correctness" signal a retreat by our entire society from fundamental notions of tolerance.'[21] And Puplick's prescription: 'If we seek to strengthen the moral fabric of society, what we need then is not less "political correctness" but more.'[22]

The recent apparent trend may in fact be contrary to the economic interests of the nation, even in the most conservative sense. It may well be a case of cultural conservatism getting in the way of economic rationalism.

There is a hard-headed economics to cultural and linguistic diversity. Many businesses are realising that Australia is a microcosm of the new, global marketplace and this is precisely the reason why a number of major multinationals have decided to locate their regional headquarters in Australia in recent years. Such organisations are beginning to recognise that diversity is not a problem— something that gets in the way of forging a cohesive workplace culture. Rather, workforces are most effective when they are as diverse as the local and global environments in which the organisation lives. The advantages include the range of language skills, communication styles, international networks, knowledge of the country and life experience that people bring to teams.

Trading on diversity is also unavoidable for Australia, as nine out of 10 of our fastest growing export markets over the past decade are non-English speaking. As the structure of our exports has changed dramatically in recent decades, with the rapid growth in highly culture-sensitive and diversity-sensitive industries such as education and tourism, we might even be so bold as to suggest that if our GDP (Gross Domestic Product) growth is now significantly ahead of most other OECD (Organisation for Economic Cooperation and Development) countries, Australia's cultural and linguistic dexterity, our local diversity and outward-looking ethos, have to be crucial factors in this success story.

Even more fundamentally, diversity is now one of the basics of our civic life. Australia has its own unique history of diversity: an immigration program that has made this perhaps the most diverse nation in the world, and the centrality of the task of completing the settlers' unfinished business with the indigenous people of this nation. Yet it also shares with the rest of the world a shift in global political orientation. Since the end of the Cold War particularly, the politics of culture, identity and nation—the politics of diversity, in other words—have taken centre stage. No nation in the world can govern unless it is able to articulate the way in which resources and wellbeing are guaranteed to different groups, including historically marginalised groups.

The Coalition needs to be reminded that, until 13 years ago, it presided in a very creative way over an extraordinary social transformation, which changed the very composition of the Australian nation and the character of the Australian people. At the end of this transformation, 40 per cent of the population has at least one parent born overseas. This is simply a different country to the ideal John Howard is enshrining—and the Coalition participated in the making of this very different country. They cannot now shirk the ongoing social redesign that is essential in a democracy. This is not just a matter of providing services and ensuring rights for all Australians, in their diversity. It also involves a continuous process of renaming and redefining the mainstream—what it means to be Australian.

So the question 'what is correct?' is a very real one. There is a certain reality—political correctness without the capitals—to the demographic growth of historical minorities; to the growing claims of minorities to cultural recognition and educational equity; to the end of the cultural and economic supremacy of the West in this phase of globalisation; and to the increasing participation of women in economic and public life. If white men and the old intellectual establishment are disoriented and disturbed—if they feel they are being told new and uncongenial truths—they are right. The world really is changing.

At the end of the twentieth century, reinventing a 'one nation' project just can't work. Two forces, the one centrifugal and the other centripetal, are together conspiring to make the nation a less and less useful cultural category and principle for cultural unification. On the one hand, globalisation means that economic and social relations are increasingly transnational and markets for commodities and culture are less identifiable in national terms. On the other hand, demographic shifts, unprecedented in their scale and accompanied by varieties of ethnic and other identity politics, mean that cultural identification is also tending to be more local and more particular than the nation-state. Traditional nationalism of the 'one nation' variety has had its day. Nation-states might well have to invent new myths to retain their legitimacy—such as the myth of a pluralism where differences are respected and granted formal equality.

A return to supposedly halcyon days of 'one nation' may be regarded as an antidote to cultural fragmentation. Yet this kind of antidote—centrally imposed, uniform, national self-definition—is only possible in many parts of the world today through repression. The ethno-nationalisms of the Balkans, which are so often used as a metaphor of the fearful consequences of diversity, are in fact the reverse: attempts to impose national cultural uniformity on populations that are diverse. 'Balkanisation' is not about differences. It is the dangerously futile attempt to create nation-states based on some imagined common cultural experience. In this sense, the conceptual basis of real 'Balkanisation' is the same as the proponents of ideas like 'one nation'. Here, while the idea of the culturally singular nation has by no means had its day, its consequences can be seen to be far from productive or peaceful.

In all probability, the sorts of historical pressures nations face at the end of the twentieth century can only be negotiated through new forms of civic pluralism. The paradox of social cohesion today—the business of making well-behaved and productive citizens—is that it must be based on a new public rhetoric of pluralism. Multiculturalism may well be performing the same social function as nationalism did in the era of local economies and autonomous nation-states. Imagining the nation now requires a different strategy, and some multiculturalisms might be found to be new ways of binding the nation for new times. So too, might be some feminisms. And so on, for all the seemingly fragmentary cultural particularisms of contemporary cultural life. And all this might happen for the most conservative of reasons in the world—to keep the wheels of commerce turning.

Notes

1 David Forman and Robert Gottliebsen, 'Taking Care of Business: Interview with John Howard', *Business Review Weekly*, 5 August 1996, pp. 42–48.

2 John Howard, 'Transcript of the Prime Minister The Hon. John Howard MP Address to the New South Wales Division of the Liberal Party Luncheon, Sydney Town Hall', Department of the Prime Minister and Cabinet, 1996.

3 John Howard, ibid.

4 John Howard, 'Transcript of Address by the Prime Minister to the Business Council of Australia, The Regent Hotel, Sydney', Department of the Prime Minister and Cabinet, 1996.

5 John Howard, 'The Australia I Believe In: The Values, Directions and Policy Priorities of a Coalition Government Outlined in 1995', Liberal–National Party Coalition Policy Document, 1995.

6 John Howard, 'Transcript of the Prime Minister The Hon. John Howard MP Adress to Youth Futures Conference, Macquarie University', Department of the Prime Minister and Cabinet, 1996.

7 *Sydney Morning Herald*, 3 August 1988.

8 ibid.

9 J. M. Fraser, Speech to the Federation of Ethnic Communities Councils Congress, 1988.

10 *Sydney Morning Herald*, 'Peacock Stirs Asian Debate', 18 March 1990, p. 1.

11 Mary Kalantzis and Bill Cope, 'A Cultural Victory for Labor', *Sydney Morning Herald*, 1993.

12 Liberal and National Party Coalition, 'Multicultural Affairs and Settlement Policy', 1996.

13 Milton Cockburn, 'A Leap of Faith', *Sydney Morning Herald*, 27 April 1996, p. 6 'Spectrum' section.

14 'Four Corners', ABC Television, 1996.

15 Paul Sheehan, ' "Too Political": Ethnic Research Unit Axed', *Sydney Morning Herald*, 1 August 1996, p. 2.

16 John Stone, 'Looking Away From Teething Problems', *Australian Financial Review*, 11 July 1996, p. 17.

17 Paul Sheehan, 'The Multicultural Myth', *Sydney Morning Herald*, 25 May 1996.

18 Maximilian Walsh, 'Labor May Have Dug its Grave with Grants', *The Age*, 31 July 1996, p. 2.

19 Geoffrey Partington, *Hasluck Versus Coombs: White Politics and Australia's Aborigines*, Quakers Hill Press, Sydney, 1996.

20 Chris Puplick, 'Truth Marching On: Equity, Political Correctness and A Fair Go For All: Address to the Equity in Vocational Education and Training Conference', Anti-Discrimination Board of New South Wales, 1996.

21 Chris Puplick, 'The World of Work: Learning to See Through Borders: Address to the 21st Annual Conference of the Careers Advisers Association of NSW', Anti-Discrimination Board of New South Wales, 1996.

22 Chris Puplick, 'Truth Marching On', op. cit.

Pauline as the thin end of the wedge

BY MARCIA LANGTON

How did the term 'political correctness', used by expatriate Australian art historian Robert Hughes in *Culture of Complaint: The Fraying of America* to characterise an argument about the demise of scholarship, come to be the clarion call of far right wing, anti-intellectual, anti-immigration, hardline elements in this country? How did this term come to be hijacked in order to trivialise the arguments of thinking Australians? Why did Australians allow this manufactured hatefulness to become a storm of political bloodletting which has brought our nation into disrepute in the region and elsewhere?

Madonna's Evita, the dance-hall girl who rises to become the wife of President Juan Peron, a Christian Dior clad star and beloved spokeswoman of the Argentinian masses, helps us to make sense of Pauline Hanson's rapid rise from club waitress to mouthpiece for the far right in fin-de-siècle Australia. Just as Juan rode to power on Evita's populist style, so has the Australian far right, in a *Strictly*

Ballroom kind of way, been elevated amongst the battlers by our own Pauline.

One part of the story began with the pre-selection of Pauline Hanson as a Liberal Party candidate, and her subsequent disendorsement by the Party just prior to the 1996 federal polling day for expressing publicly her unacceptable—at least until then—racist views.

Prior to this time, successive federal governments had almost rid the nation's image of its associations with the period of the White Australia policy. Hanson, a White Australia advocate, had lost her place on the local Ipswich Council in south-east Queensland after its April 1995 amalgamation with Moreton Council. On 2 August 1995, Hanson joined the local Bremer branch of the Liberal Party and, after three months, was pre-selected to contest the then safe Labor seat of Oxley in the forthcoming federal election.

On 12 February 1996, Hanson achieved her first national headlines with claims that Aborigines were themselves responsible for racist sentiments expressed about them. Two days later, she was disendorsed by the Queensland division of the Liberal Party with the assent of party leader John Howard. Her racist abuse of Aborigines and 'Asians' included the electoral stance that she would fight for the white community, 'the immigrants, Italians, Greeks, whoever, it really [doesn't] matter—anyone apart from Aborigines and Torres Strait Islanders', she said while in Canberra.

She won the seat with a 19 per cent swing and drew to her cause a national following, including politicians, such as Noel Crichton-Browne, and 'shock jock' talk-back radio hosts, such as Alan Jones and Stan Zemanek.

At the time of her disendorsement, the ballot papers had already been printed, reading 'Pauline Hanson—Liberal', and hundreds of fliers and posters had been distributed throughout the seat of Oxley. Adam Indikt, writing for the *Australian/Israel Review*, reported the observations of Les Scott, the then sitting ALP member, and David Pullen, the candidate for the Australian Democrats in Oxley, who noted that 'the Liberal machine was still openly assisting the Hanson campaign'. They described how members of the Bremer branch of the Liberal Party distributed Hanson Independent how-to-vote cards outside polling booths with one hand, and Liberal Senate how-to-vote cards with the other. Les Scott also described how the president of the Bremer branch scrutineered for Hanson on election day, and how other members of the branch handed out Hanson Independent how-to-vote cards.[1]

On 6 March, four days after Hanson won Oxley, John Pasquarelli, from the office of Graeme Campbell (who had himself been disendorsed by the ALP), came on board as her assistant to liaise with the media and to give her political advice.

In her maiden speech to the Australian Parliament, Hanson detailed further her vision of 'ONE PEOPLE, ONE NATION, ONE FLAG!':

I believe we are in danger of being swamped by Asians. Between 1984 and 1995, 40 per cent of all migrants into this country were of Asian origin. They have their own culture and religion, form ghettos [sic] and do not assimilate. Of course, I will be called racist, but if I can invite who I want into my home, then I should have the right to have a say in who comes into my country. A truly multicultural country can NEVER be strong or united and the world is full of failed and tragic examples, ranging from Ireland to Bosnia, to Africa, and closer to home, Papua New Guinea. America and Great Britain are currently paying the price.

Mr Acting Speaker, Arthur Calwell was a great Australian and Labor leader and it is a pity that there are not men of his stature sitting on the Opposition benches today. Arthur Calwell said, and I quote, *"Japan, India, Burma, Ceylon and every new African nation are fiercely anti-white and anti one another. Do we want or need any of these people here? I am one red-blooded Australian who says NO and who speaks for 90 per cent of Australians"*.

I have no hesitation in echoing the words of Arthur Calwell!

Mr Acting Speaker, there is light at the end of the tunnel and there are solutions. If this government wants to be fair dinkum, then it must stop kowtowing to financial markets, international organisatons, world bankers, investment companies and big business people . . .

Mr Acting Speaker, time is running out . . . Because of our resources and our position in the world, we won't have a say because neighbouring countries such as Japan with 250 million people, China (1.2 billion), India (1 billion), Indonesia (250 million) and Malaysia (300 million) are well aware of our resources and potential. WAKE UP AUSTRALIA BEFORE IT IS TOO LATE!!![2]

Perhaps one source of inspiration for Hanson—or Pasquarelli—was *The New Citizen*, the extreme right-wing newspaper which publishes the views of the La Rouchians.

The front-page headline of the February–March 1995 edition screamed 'Global financial collapse underway', above a lead paragraph claiming that:

> Around the world, leading people—bankers and political people—who, up until a few weeks or months ago would have either denied, or did deny, and would have rejected or even ridiculed [Lyndon La Rouche's] forecast on the present monetary situation, now are saying that the entire international monetary and financial system is in the process of disintegration. Not just collapse, but disintegration.[3]

So what has led to this dire situation covered extensively in *The New Citizen*? It is more than interesting that the perceived causes are much as Mrs Hanson would have us believe. An editorial in the same edition asks:

> Which Way for Australia?
>   This issue . . . presents two antagonistic visions of the future of our country. The first is that of . . . multiculturalism, and a proposed "separate Aboriginal nation". As we documented in this issue, plans have advanced very far to rewrite our Constitution towards these ends by the time of our Centenary in 2001. The second vision is that of an optimistic, growing Australia integrated around great economic development projects . . .
>   . . .
>   It is now time, once again, to rise to the challenge which history places before us . . .Unless we sweep aside the oligarchy's nonsensical, but evil, doctrines of radical environmentalism, multiculturalism, and a "separate

Aboriginal nation", and implement those urgently required measures of national banking, protective tariffs, debt moratoria, etc. ... Australia as we know it will be swept from the pages of history.[4]

The New Citizen also argues in a small article under the heading 'Are Aborigines Human Beings?' that 'Western Judeo–Christian civilisation is the highest form of culture to have emerged on this planet; to deny Aborigines the chance to participate in that culture, is to deny them their essential humanity . . .'[5]. Variations of this argument, which attempt to rehabilitate assimilationist thinking about Aborigines, have been espoused by Ron Brunton of the Conservative think-tank, the Institute of Public Affairs, and by Geoffrey Partington, author of *Hasluck v. Coombs*, launched last year by the Minister for Aboriginal Affairs, Senator John Herron.

The stance of *The New Citizen* resounds in Hanson's view of the way forward for Australia—an Australia she perceives as being economically and socially undermined by present policies concerning cultural diversity, policies built on ideas that have been labelled by Hanson and her fellow travellers as 'political correctness'.

Evita Peron reinvented herself as the sartorially resplendent patroness of the poor to distract the attention of the struggling masses from their country's downward-spiralling economy and conditions under the repressive Junta. Hanson's effect is to distract the attention of battlers from the difficulty of stretching their paypackets to meet basic needs by the use of simplistic, white supremacist ideology, and to concentrate their anger on the wrong, but soft, targets.

The aim, witting or unwitting, of those who use the term 'political correctness' has been to silence debate and give priority to ideas about what constitutes acceptable Australian 'mainstream', or dominant, identity and views. The term swept to prominence as a key word in national debate with the resurgence of 'race' politics. At a time when it seemed that cultural and historical differences could be freely expressed by the diverse Australian citizenry; when Aborigines and post-World War II immigrants had finally desisted from the polite mimicry of what had been interpreted as desirable Anglo–Australian forms of sociality; when it seemed that principles of fairness, racial and sexual equality, civil and human rights standards, and equality of opportunity for all might become entrenched in our political way of life; when it seemed that all of this could be taken for granted, a deep cultural change has placed these values in jeopardy. The cultural change has been led by a few individuals, the self-styled victims of 'political correctness', strategically tapping into the deep-seated vein of Australian racism that has been muted by post-Whitlam identity politics.

During the 1996 federal election campaign in Australia, 'race' politics—the cynical use for electoral purposes of community superstitions and suspicions based on folkloric beliefs concerning physical and intellectual characteristics and genetic inheritance—were the most blatant, crude and divisive since the white worker riots against indentured Pacific Island labour in the pre-Federation period. Hanson was a godsend to the Right in the run-up to the election because she articulated in the language of the battlers the case that respectable politicians could not. She created a space for those who preface their xenophobic statements with 'I'm not racist but . . .' while Liberal Party politicians and candidates needed only to remain silent to indicate their assent to her views, thus benefiting from the huge electoral swings to their side of politics. In the provinces, the leaders were far more overt. For instance, Northern Territory Chief Minister Shane Stone set the tone for a Territory election by publicly describing Aboriginal patrician Gumatj clan leader and Chairman of the Northern Land Council, Galarrwuy Yunupingu, in epithets such as 'despicable', 'whingeing, whining black' and 'treacherous'.

This strategy of cultural warfare or 'wedge politics' has been only recently introduced into our once unworldly, rather innocent approach to electoral campaigning. Some suspect that Liberal Party apparatchiks learnt the dark arts of dividing the community on 'race' issues from the Republicans in the United States of America. 'Wedge politics' promotes a campaign of fear and loathing, based on a strategically chosen issue, before a fascinated media in order to polarise the electorate and scare swinging voters to scurry to the right (or the left, as the case may be) in fear—fear, to describe some of the examples used in America, that black murderers and rapists are not being given life sentences or the death penalty, or that black single mothers are coming out of the ghettos in tens of thousands, driving the welfare budget up and placing outrageous burdens on the (white) taxpayer.

It was possible to interpret the efforts of several columnists in the Hindmarsh Island saga as 'wedge politics'. By foregrounding complaints by certain ex-mission Aboriginal women that an application by some Ngarrindjeri women to obtain protection over an area jeopardised by a bridge development was based on 'fabricated' claims about sacredness, Christopher Pearson, Chris Kenny and others were able to sow seeds of doubt about the authenticity of any case involving Aboriginal religiosity in the urbanised south. This may cast doubt upon any such applications under the Aboriginal and Torres Strait Islander Heritage Act.

The Hindmarsh Bridge case was not a land claim. It was an application for protection of a sacred site under that Act. Such an application, if successful, cannot change the underlying land tenure, and can only impose a restriction on the use of the land, much as a heritage order does.

Throughout the years that this dispute about a sacred site has been before the public gaze, there has been a persistent undertow: that it is somehow invalid—outrageous even—that Progress, as represented by the Hindmarsh Island Bridge proposal, should be held up by Superstition, as represented by the application by Ngarrindjeri women. Newspaper cartoons have made much of this primordial conflict in Australian society, sometimes with intelligent and amusing representations of the Rainbow Serpent weaving its way through Australian politics, but more often with derisive depictions of blackskinned characters with wide eyes and flared nostrils engaged in a lurid political sideshow, depictions heavily charged with popular imagery of indigenous people as evolutionary oddities from an earlier epoch.

In Australia, where Aboriginal people are less than two per cent of the population yet have an imprisonment rate of nearly 30 times that of other Australians, and where Aboriginal people are more likely to be in jail for failing to pay a fine than for a major offence, the manufacture of the bogeyman requires more imagination and creativity than in the United States, where slavery and social separation of blacks from whites by legal mechanisms is very recent, where civil disorder and riots sparked by civil rights abuses are capable of flaring up at any provocation, and where African–Americans are 20 per cent of the population. There the ghettos form the netherworld of the white imagination. Here in Australia the fear is more indirect, more psychological than physical, more surrogate than visceral. It is difficult to argue rationally, in the cold light of day, with all the facts at hand, that Aborigines present any threat at all to decent, law-abiding, God-fearing white Australians.

Identity, not prosperity, is what is really at stake for Australians in the political psychodramas that cast Aborigines as a demonic threat.

Pauline Hanson's sweeping success as an Independent and her subsequent inflammatory statements have created an environment where extreme right-wing views, including overt white supremacist statements, are becoming acceptable within the normal discourse of Australian society. Hanson, whether she knows it or not, has become the publicly acceptable face of the extreme right-wing group, the League of Rights. The League of Rights is the equivalent of the United Kingdom's National Front, and attempts to masks its reactionary agenda by campaigning through mainstream media and politics.

Hanson drew praise from League of Rights leader Eric Butler, who dubbed her 'The Hanson Miracle' and 'The Hanson Bombshell' and who has distributed copies of her maiden speech to thousands of supporters nationally. Jewish political observers have noted the growing success of a right-wing extremism in Australian political life since the last federal election campaign. In *The Australian/Israel Review*, Adam Indikt revealed that:

> Hanson has emerged as one of the most revered figures in the rejuvenated far right network in Australia. *The Review* has learned that during the March federal election, she directed preferences to Victor Robb, a well-known neo-Nazi extremist, who also ran as an Independent candidate for the Federal seat of Oxley.
>
> Robb is the former secretary of the Queensland branch of the neo-Nazi National Front of Australia.
>
> . . .
>
> Victor Robb advocates bizarre economic views which include the end of the banking system in order to "bring about the salvation of civilisation". During the Federal election Hanson directed her preferences to Robb . . . he also directed preferences to Hanson and "thoroughly supports Pauline Hanson's views." One of Robb's election advertisements called for the "anti-Asianisation of Australia".[6]

After her electoral success, Hanson and her supporters received standing ovations at meetings around the country at which they peddled their divisive notions of a white Australia, an end to "Asian" immigration, and an end to programs aimed at overcoming the disadvantages of indigenous people.

* * *

During the nationwide fuss stirred up by Mrs Hanson, the new Prime Minister, John Howard, gave a speech to the State Council meeting of the New South Wales Liberal

Party on 20 April 1996, during which he outlined his views on 'political correctness':

> One of the things that characterised Australia before 2 March was the growing tide of what some people have called social censorship, at what other people have called political correctness, and what I would call a plain, old-fashioned assault on free speech and free political debate. We have reached a state in this country where it was not possible for people reasonably and moderately and decently to even talk about certain subjects without being branded with all sorts of reprehensible labels and descriptions, and to the extent that the change of government has lifted that pall, has changed that atmosphere, has once again emboldened people to talk—and I use these words deliberately again, moderately and decently but openly—about all sorts of subjects in the Australian community, then I think that is an extremely welcome development because the last 13 years were ... a period of time in which the Labor Party leadership sought to rewrite the history of this country.[7]

Columnist and Director of the Sydney Institute Gerard Henderson has found a probable origin for the term 'political correctness' in an article by Dinesh D'Souza, writing for *On the Issues*:

> The term "political correctness" seems to have originated in the early part of this century, when it was employed by various species of Marxists to describe and enforce conformity to preferred ideological positions ... Eventually the term dropped out of the lexicon, only to be revived

in the 1980s, when it came to apply to the assorted ideologies for the late 1960s and early 1970s: black consciousness and black power, feminism, homosexual rights and, to a lesser degree, pacifism, environmentalism, and so on . . .

The first article about political correctness in a national publication was Richard Bernstein's *New York Times* feature, "The Rising Hegemony of the Politically Correct". Published on 29 October 1990, the article suggested that even though some of the preferred terms "are not used in utter seriousness," nevertheless an "unofficial ideology" was generating to conform among students and faculty at American Universities.[8]

Henderson rightly points out, as Robert Hughes had earlier, that political correctness—the sacrifice of scholarly standards of investigation and verification to fashionable and contemporary notions of standards and conventions etcetera—was a real problem on some North American campuses in the late 1980s and early 1990s. However, Henderson goes on to note:

> . . . no similar phenomenon was experienced in Australia— on university campuses or elsewhere . . . The fact is that there is genuine political debate in Australia. Geoffrey Blainey proves the point. He speaks throughout Australia, his thoughts find expression in the mainstream media and he is one of Australia's most successful authors. If PC really prevailed, this could not have occurred. Nor would John Howard have become Prime Minister of Australia— with the support of almost all newspaper editorials and with a relatively sympathetic media.[9]

Robert Hughes's timely critique of political correctness in the United States is all well and fine for the literati, and it is important to be vigilant, to continue to critique 'political correctness' and to provide the antidote to undergraduate rejection of standards of scholarship on the grounds of misunderstood sentiments concerning feminism and racism. But for the average punter, political correctness means what Graeme Campbell means in the introduction to his book *Australia Betrayed*, in which he argues that political correctness is identical with support for 'multicultralism, hard-line feminism and Asianisation'.[10]

The Prime Minister's decision to dispute the new Australian history—one based on research and scholarship[11]—clarified the issues considerably. The history of the conqueror versus the history of the vanquished became a hot political issue even in the highest political office in the land.

'Our children are taught that ... some of the school curricula go close to teaching children that we have a racist, bigoted past', said the Prime Minister in 1996's Sir Robert Menzies lecture. (It should not be forgotten that the key intellectuals employed by the Institute of Public Affairs had for some years been shaping such ideological counters to the New Left critique.)

It was inevitable that those who feel representative of what they imagine to be the Australian version of the Tory view of the world would revolt against the threat to an assumed Australian identity—the Australia of the Anzacs, of Arnott's Iced Vo-Vos, and King Gee brand blue overalls. The new Australian history that emerged from the universities from the 1960s onwards, as Henry Reynolds, Ann McGrath, Ann Curthoys, Heather Goodall, Peter Read, Lyndall Ryan, Tim Rowse, and Bain Attwood, among others published their theses, resulted in accounts of our past that were astonishing in their divergence from the school textbook accounts of Jackey Jackey and nameless spear-wielding 'natives'. From the work of these historians, a view of Australia's past had taken shape like a giant jigsaw puzzle, each piece a memorandum, a letter, a diary entry or other documentary fragment, and each which revealed something of the terrible truth. Anthropologists, such as the late W. E. H. Stanner, and linguists wrote back from the field documenting fascinating and complex grammars and kinship and ideational systems. These discoveries fed into a growing cultural movement which in Australia emerged from The Sydney Push in the 1960s, and expanded during the Vietnam War protests, the leftist critique of Cold War politics, and the poststructuralist questions that reframed ideas about society and the individual, the identity/cultural diversity debates, race, gender, environmental justice, discourse, and power. But as the ABC Television series 'Frontier' reminds us, ideas concerning indigenous rights are not a spin-off of these issue movements as sometimes proposed, but predate all of these developments by at least a century.

The view has been proffered that white Australians should not feel guilty about the actions of previous generations. Pauline Hanson said she drew the line 'when told I must pay and continue paying for something that happened over 200 years ago'.[12]

It is necessary to deal with the core assumption of this statement, because it expresses a belief that many people hold, including people of consequence such as the Prime Minister of Australia. But people who have read texts by reliable historians are aware that the *somethings* that happened to Aboriginal people—say, for instance, frontier violence—were still occurring in the 1920s as documented in the cases of the Coniston and the Forrest River massacres. But more critical to this national debate is the problem that the *somethings* that are happening to Aboriginal people *now* are still not perceived by most of the politicians, researchers, bureaucrats, opinion leaders, talk-back radio hosts, and members of the public to be a direct consequence of those events that took place during the frontier period proper.

This has been the challenge for the Council of Reconciliation: how to foster an understanding amongst tion.AAustralians that the disadvantages suffered by indigenous Australians today can be rectified by policies and programs that pay due regard to the historical cause of those disadvantages. At the same time, there are few Aboriginal people who have considered these problems seriously who would deny that there must be an effort made by Aboriginal people to put the mark of history behind us and refuse to be victims of the past.

But merely having such a desire will not magically prevent the dull hand of ignorance from stifling the innovations that must be made in this area by governments and by ordinary people. A good example of this problem is the rising rates of imprisonment of indigenous people: how do we convince the magistrates, sergeants of police and beat coppers that sending minor offenders, especially juveniles, to gaols and institutions is counter-productive and inhuman, and that they can and ought to use other strategies to redirect offenders to alternative correctional programs?

Our political leaders, touchy about advising their

constituencies of the need to acknowledge past wrongs, are hoping to secure reconciliation via the back door—telling Aboriginal Australians to turn a blind eye to the past and focus on the future because it is expedient for politicians for them to do so.

The response of the populist pork-barrellers from all political quarters to this approach to reconciliation lately has been to dismiss its proponents as members of the so-called black armband brigade, foot soldiers for the view that Australians should be riddled with guilt about the past. Speaking in the Sir Robert Menzies Lecture on 18 November 1996, Prime Minister Howard said:

> This black armband view of our past reflects the belief that most Australian history since 1788 has been little more than a disgraceful story of imperialism, exploitation, racism, sexism and other forms of discrimination.
>
> I take a very different view. I believe that the balance sheet of our history is one of heroic achievement and that we have achieved much more as a nation of which we can be proud than of which we should be ashamed.[13]

But history should not be a selective grab bag from which are drawn only those events deemed to support national pride. Australia cannot on the one hand use the highlights of its history as a backdrop for our contemporary culture, and yet ignore as irrelevant the darker side of its past. If the past is irrelevant, then it is irrelevant in its entirety. Aboriginal and Torres Strait Islander people have contested the claims of, for instance, some in the Victorian Returned Soldiers, Sailors and Airmen's Imperial League, who have asserted that Aborigines did not play a role in the defence of Australia during the various wars in which Australians fought, and so they should therefore be grateful that they now live in a free country. This, too, was an unsubstantiated assumption: in fact, thousands of Aboriginal men and women have fought in every war in which the Commonwealth of Australia has made a contribution. Australians have been slow to acknowledge the courage and sacrifice made by the first peoples of this land in wars, but the acknowledgment has come, reluctantly. In 1995, the last living members of the Northern Territory Special Reconnaissance Unit, which was made up of Yolngu men, reunited with their superior officers at the Anzac Day Memorial in Darwin to contemplate their war effort and remember those who were no longer with them. From the remotest Aboriginal hearth to the cities, there is cause to commemorate their sacrifices—sacrifices made by loyal Australian men and women who had no regard for colour. They served often without pay, without adequate food and equipment, and in circumstances of racial intolerance, as the late Captain Reginald Walter Saunders, first Aboriginal officer in the Australian Defence Forces, documented in his biography. Today, Aborigines comprise more than a quarter of the membership of NORFORCE, which is responsible for patrolling about a quarter of the Australian landmass.[14]

* * *

The 'race' debate amplified by Pauline Hanson resulted in a rash of reports around the country of verbal and physical abuse directed towards Aboriginal and other non-white people. Some Anglo-Australians have been moved to object. The Anglican Archbishop of Sydney, Dr Harry Goodhew, spoke out against racism, and former Prime Minister Malcolm Fraser warned that the current 'race' debate is 'extraordinarily dangerous for the future of Australia'.

One of the core assumptions in this debate is that the toxic relationship between many Australians with a British background and indigenous people must be the only litmus test for cultural relations. While it is true that most bureaucrats, academics, politicians, teachers, policemen, doctors, and dentists—the professionals and the governors—do have such a British background, a large number of Australians do not. The cultural diversity of Australians is a significant social fact of modern life, and it should be of great concern to Aboriginal people that their relations with people of non-British backgrounds is developed. What do recent immigrants know about Aboriginal people? A concern to answer this question might be more important than our responses to Mrs Hanson. The way in which she used statistics in her assertions is a problem that must be taken up by all those she casts as undesirable: for example, the figures she cites about 'Asian' immigration include any immigrant from every country east of the Black Sea on the Asian continent; thus Turks are counted as 'Asians'. The reply to such statements must come from all those people who have been 'orientalised', to misuse distinguished Middle Eastern scholar Edward Said's idea.

But in the way that nouveau colonists who arrive in Australia's northern provincial cities learn the local etiquette of 'race' relations at barbecues, education about Aboriginal people continues to come from the wrong sources. Perhaps these tens of thousands of new(er) Australians could avoid repeating the mistakes of their British predecessors in their relations with indigenous people if

Aboriginal people were to engage with a wider represen-
tation of Australians, and not simply to the imagined centre
of Australian political life—the former British powerbase.

Nations have traditionally looked to their political
leaders to point the way, to continually strive to see the big
picture when individuals with a range of vested interests
cannot or will not do so. As Australia's current crop of
political leaders fail this test in relation to racial tolerance
and reconciliation, are they now to be taught a lesson by
other leaders? United States President Bill Clinton, during
his visit to Australia late in 1996, urged Australians to:

> Think of the terrible spectacle we have seen in Africa in
> the last few days ... think of what it's like in the Holy
> Land ... think of what it is like in Bosnia where there is
> literally, biologically, no difference between the Serbs, the
> Croats, the Muslims ...
>
> There is a lot of evidence that we can all do better
> than that, and when the world comes to Sydney [for the
> 2000 Olympics] they will see that. So think about that.[15]

Contrast this with the bipartisan resolution passed by
the Australian Parliament on 30 October 1996, which,
while ostensibly reaffirming the commitment to reconciliation, left a great deal unsaid.

There is a very real danger that loose talk about 'political correctness' will legitimise the old paternalist era when
Aborigines were institutionalised as Wards of the State in
order to 'assimilate' them. Until the referendum of 1967,
the Commonwealth had no role in Aboriginal affairs,
except in the Northern Territory, and thus there was no
protection of Aboriginal rights; each indigenous population

was at the whim of its State's provincial administrations. Aboriginal people did not have the right to vote until, at the end of this era, each State jurisdiction was forced by international censure to enfranchise indigenous people. Aboriginal death rates were among the highest recorded in the world—and have since then only declined slowly. For nearly 30 years, most informed observers of Aboriginal affairs have recognised that no good can come of institutionalising Aboriginal people as mendicants, or socio-economic political prisoners, as Aboriginal rights lawyer and Mabo and Wik negotiator Noel Pearson so aptly puts it.

It is difficult to avoid the conclusion that the culmination of years of maturation in our political and social debate—a pride in our cultural diversity—has been transformed into a hypocritical gloss on national economic goals by the failure of the Prime Minister and other political leaders to convincingly repudiate the zealotry of Mrs Hanson.

In the film version of the musical of the *real life* story, Madonna's Evita trills pathetically 'Have I said too much?' As Pauline Hanson follows her shooting-star trajectory, this is a question she is unlikely to ask herself, but one that might usefully be asked on her behalf by some of our politicians and opinion leaders if they care to survey the damage in her wake.

Notes

1 *The Australian/Israel Review*, October/November 1996, p. 7.
2 Hanson, Pauline, Member for Oxley, *Maiden Speech* [to Parliament of Australia], from photocopy of original, 1996: 9–14.

3 *The New Citizen*, February–March 1995 issue, p. 1.

4 ibid, p. 2.

5 ibid, p. 14.

6 *The Australian/Israel Review*, October/November 1997, p. 7.

7 Cited in "Political Correctness" in *Gerard Henderson's Media Watch*, Issue 36, No. 2, 1996, p. 5.

8 As cited in Gerard Henderson, ibid., p. 12; *On the Issues* is published by the American Enterprise Institute.

9 ibid, p. 12.

10 ibid, p. 4.

11 The most notable representative of the historians who have challenged the 'History of the Empire' Tory school of thought on Australian history is Professor Henry Reynolds, author of many influential texts, most notably *Law of the Land*, which inspired the questions to the High Court in *The Wik People v. The State of Queensland & Ors* and *The Thayorre People v. The State of Queensland & Ors*.

12 *Australian*, 11 September 1996, p. 2.

13 As reported the *Australian*, 19 November 1996, p. 13.

14 See, for instance, Desmond Ball (ed.), *Aborigines in the Defence of Australia*, Australian National University Press, Botany, NSW, 1991.

15 As quoted in the *Australian*, 22 November 1996, p. 1.

Back to the Brady Bunch

BY CATHARINE LUMBY

If 1996 was any guide, Lewis Carroll was born too early—we're living in times which rival Alice's Adventures in Wonderland.

Times when marginality is always a shelf above or below the spot we left it last. And when 'political correctness' always means precisely what its critics want it to mean. A world where feminists, lesbians and gays, and Aboriginal people can be attacked at breakfast for promoting divorce, debauchery and social division (Not Enough Rules) and pilloried over afternoon tea for imposing fascist restrictions on what can be said, fondled or mined (Too Many Rules).

Of course, if Carroll *was* living now, his alter ego, Charles Dodson, would probably be busy explaining himself to Kay Martin. The sexually ambiguous photographs Dodson took of Alice Liddell, his dark-eyed child muse, look like invitations to a public lynching in the current paedophile-alert climate.

But then we live in deeply paranoid times. Times which

twitch with the energies of diverse moral panics. Times when the enemy wears many faces but the good guys are instantly recognisable: the Decent, Hardworking, Ordinary Australians under siege from the Lunatic Fringe. Times when conservatives detect 'elitist' extremists behind every challenge to the status quo, and when John Howard can accuse his opponents of 'McCarthyite' tactics. Times when defending the family means attacking anyone who fails the nuclear test. Perverse times indeed.

Even if political correctness is no longer the mantra it was, traditionally disadvantaged groups are still being accused of making unreasonable claims on 'ordinary' Australians. It's an idea used by conservatives to stake their own claim to minority status.

In her infamous maiden speech to parliament, Pauline Hanson claimed that Aboriginals enjoy privileges denied to other Australians and blamed political correctness for this purported oppression of the majority. 'Ordinary' Australians, Hanson argues, have been sidelined by marginal interests—that is, People With Funny-Coloured Skin. It's easy to dismiss Hanson's rhetoric as the rabid racism it undoubtedly is, but the opposition she makes between 'ordinary' people and minority groups is, in fact, fundamental to the broader debate about the 'relaxed' and 'comfortable' society we're supposedly becoming.

Whether the issue is feminism, Aboriginal land rights or the teaching of cultural studies in universities, many conservatives on both the left and right are busy claiming that the voices of reasonable people are being silenced by extremists. That they're not against change, they're just against things going Too Far or against special interest groups dominating the agenda—that they'd simply like a restoration of what Pauline Hanson called 'common sense'.

This claim to the middle ground is echoed in the growing debate about family values in Australia. If the mythical 'average' Ordinary Australian is the standard by which anyone who wants to change the status quo can be judged a ratbag extremist, then the family is the unit by which 'normal' attitudes to gender and sexuality can be measured. Feminists who simply want the right to education or a job are one thing, but women who challenge the foundations of traditional family life are something else. As radio personality Terry Lane puts it, they're 'the small, really embittered minority' who show that feminism's 'pendulum has swung as far as it is going to and eventually it will settle back'.[1]

If the debate about the needs of Ordinary Australians revolves around fears that our public sphere is changing too quickly, the family values debate is its equally paranoid private-sphere mirror.

* * *

Like the phrase 'political correctness', 'family values' is an import from US political debate. And like other political buzzwords, 'family values' is one which manages to be everywhere and nowhere simultaneously. Everyone's talking about family values—but no one seems terribly sure what they are.

In America, family values have become a political mantra which transcends party lines—in the 1996 Presidential election both Dole and Clinton put the family at the centre of their campaign rhetoric. What they *mean* by 'family', though, is another matter.

For the Republican Party and, more importantly, for the religious right who now make up 25 per cent of the GOP, the 'family' represents the moral centre of America—it's the place where spiritual and political order begins. In fundamentalist terms, that means a top-down patriarchal chain of authority starting with God-the-Father. And it means a gendered division of labour in which women are cast as creatures of nature and nurture and men are creatures of culture and competition.

North American social conservatives don't pussyfoot around when it comes to expressing their views on feminism. According to Christian Coalition founder Pat Robertson, feminists 'encourage women to leave their husbands, kill their children and become lesbians'.

Bill Clinton has tried to house family values in a broader church. His wife, the much-savaged feminist icon, Hillary Clinton, summed it up when she told the 1996 Democratic convention: 'Of course, parents first and foremost are responsible for their children. But we are all responsible for ensuring that children are raised in a nation that doesn't just talk about valuing family values but acts in ways that values families.' Even two years ago, she might have voiced what her comment about families implies: that in the US family values has become a code word—and an alibi—for dismantling State protection of the poorest women and children. But then Clinton himself has been pushed so far to the right that he signed a welfare bill which effectively dismantled the social safety net for families in poverty.

In Australia, one of the first signs that the family-values virus had infected politics came in 1992, when then Prime Minister Paul Keating claimed Hollywood film violence was infiltrating society and causing 'terrible child murders'. Expressing concern for his own daughters, aged 13, 11 and seven, he said they were 'at the age where they are being subjected to very explicit violence' on television. One movie had 'quite upset' his youngest daughter and his older children were at an age where violent media was a 'bad influence' on them.[2] Mr Keating's references to his family placed his concerns about the media squarely within a traditional paternalistic framework. The media represents the corrupting and dangerous forces of an outside world from which the prime minister's children—and by extension, all Australians as people who were in his executive care—need to be protected.

Keating's attempt to pit family values against the evil commercial empire of popular culture puts him in good conservative company. In 1994, Pope John Paul attacked television as a major threat to family life, saying it glorified sex and violence and recklessly spread false values. Challenging parents to 'simply turn the set off', the Pope said television spread 'degrading values by broadcasting pornography and graphic depiction of brutal violence'.[3] And Republican Party candidate Bob Dole launched his 1996 Presidential campaign by attacking the entertainment industry for 'mainstreaming deviancy'. 'A line has been crossed,' he said. 'Not just of taste, but of human dignity and decency.' He went on to divide popular music and films into two groups—'friendly to families' and 'nightmares of depravity'.[4]

John Howard has since taken the Australian family values debate further to the right. A former member of the Lyons Forum (a group of Coalition MPs with views on the family not dissimilar to those of the American religious right) Howard made family values central to his successful 1996 electoral campaign.

But where exactly does this imported family values rhetoric leave us? Or more specifically, where does it leave the Australian family? It's a question which begs another. Exactly what *is* the contemporary family in Australia?

Professor of Demography at the Australian National University, Peter McDonald, gives us some idea with his 1995 survey.[5] Premarital sex is widespread—more than 50 per cent of people live together before getting married. About one-third of marriages end in divorce. Most mothers work—40 per cent with a child under five and 70 per cent when a child goes to school. One in four children are born out of wedlock. And many more same-sex couples are out of the closet and interested in parenting.

On the face of it, these figures appear to confirm claims that family life is in ruins—Mike-and-Carol-Brady World it isn't. But then why focus on the negatives of the contemporary social landscape? Why not consider the gains heralded by these statistics—positive changes, like more involved male parenting, more flexible working lives for men and women, less pressure to stay in unhappy relationships, and a society which is generally less conformist and more tolerant of diversity.

When you strip away the moral hype, in fact, it's clear that what we're facing is not a *loss* of family values, but an intensely political debate over what those values ought to be. And who's setting the agenda. Or to put it in starker terms, it's a debate over what we ought to value about the family itself.

*   *   *

In liberal democracies, the family has been the traditional counterweight to civil society. It's a haven from public life—the domain of love, interdependence, sexuality and nurturing. Civil society, on the other hand, is the realm of politics, work, competition and independence. It's a divide which mapped a sexual division of labour—men bring home the bacon and women cook it.

Since the late 1960s, though, this white-picket-fence vision of domestic bliss has been rapidly coming unstuck. Across the Western world, traditional gender roles are breaking down—and with them, the rigid separation of public and family life. Issues formerly considered private, like child-rearing, sexuality, domestic violence and relationships, are popping up in the public domain, while public-sphere issues like politics and economics have conversely penetrated the private domain, in the shape of feminism and paid child-care.

It's an erosion of patriarchal business-as-usual, which you might expect feminists and their political allies to embrace. In fact, many on the left are proving every bit as concerned about the collapse of family values as their counterparts on the right.

Ex-*OZ* publisher Richard Neville is just one of a number of old radicals who have indulged in some public recanting. In an article in the now defunct *Independent Monthly* headlined 'Kill Culture'[6], he told the story of how a three-year-old child he took into a video store became distraught after glimpsing a shooting on the monitor. Neville reflected: 'It took about 10 minutes for the tot to recover her equanimity ... but I'm still brooding'. The incident is an invitation for Neville to pose a series of sanctimonious questions about the state of contemporary culture and its potential to lead us into 'a collective slough of narcissism, despair and bloodshed'.

Neville's indiscriminate attacks on popular culture bear an uncomfortable resemblance to Bob Dole's. Both men are prey to the same fears about what Neville calls 'this unravelling world'. Both think the mass media and youth culture are destabilising contemporary society. Both argue we need to exercise self-restraint and restore some order. As Neville puts it 'This is not a time for degeneracy but regeneration, a time to reconstruct, not deconstruct'.

But moral panic over popular culture isn't just a bloke thing—a number of senior Australian feminists have formed a coalition with the far right and, in the process, they've provided fundamentalists with a rhetorical smoke-screen for their conservative views on women and families. Here's Senator Brian 'Blue Stocking' Harradine, for instance, objecting in the Senate to non-violent erotica: '... much of the X-rated material treats women as sexual commodities to arouse the sexual desire of its targeted audience and reduces persons to objects or occasions or sexual pleasure'.[7]

On the face of it, Harradine's objection to X-rated material is perfectly in line with popular feminist objections. But his views on abortion and a range of other feminist issues make it clear that the senator's objections to women being treated as 'sexual commodities' flow from a religious and deeply paternalistic view of the female role.

The claim that violent and sexually explicit media is damaging children and contributing to the breakdown of the family has become a familiar meeting ground for feminists and social conservatives. Liberal Party Senator Hedley Chapman summed up this family values view when he praised a new classification bill for exhibiting 'a commitment by the government to ensuring that community standards and family values are not usurped by the ever-increasing flood of pornography and unacceptable material which seems to be creeping into every facet of life in Australia'.[8]

This family values rhetoric fits well with a moralistic and reactionary strain of maternalism which lies at the heart of pro-censorship feminism and which endorses a vision of society where right-minded feminists will act as de facto spiritual parents to the rest of us (with the aid of State power). The aim is to institutionalise the ethical values of a particular section of the feminist movement, using a combination of surveillance and discipline. In other words, we'll be allowed access to sexually explicit material when we've all been properly schooled in the higher feminist ethical understanding of human sexuality. When we've learnt to want erotica, not pornography.

The problem is that notions of 'real' sexuality, like 'real' women or 'real' life, are inevitably grounded in coercive notions of what it means to be normal or right with the world. And that's precisely the point at which pro-censorship feminism links back up with a religious, fundamentalist family values agenda and, unwittingly, also aligns itself with the views of the very people who accuse feminists of imposing their elitist views on the Ordinary Australians.

*   *   *

Social conservatives on both the right and the left talk about tradition, stability, self-control and discipline as if they're the only values that matter. But as anyone trying to juggle the pressures of work, a relationship and young children knows, families require other values too—like tolerance, flexibility, a healthy respect for our own failings, and an ability to live with differences.

One of the unofficial anthems of Sydney's Gay and Lesbian Mardi Gras is the disco hit 'We Are Family'. It's a song which expresses a vision of family fundamental to many gays and lesbians—the idea that family begins with community. With friends, lovers and the people who frequent the same neighbourhoods and share your values, lifestyle and sexual preferences.

Nuclear families are built on a series of fixed relationships, with the husband and wife at the centre. The community-as-family notion is far more fluid, anticipating a wide variety of liaisons—lovers, old friends, new acquaintances—and a fluctuating sense of where the community begins and ends. At times of public celebration, like the Mardi Gras, the borders of the gay and lesbian scene are open to members of the broader community, but at times of crisis they are far more carefully policed.

At its best, though, the gay and lesbian community describes a space in which identity isn't based on a reactive Us versus Them model. In queer culture, for example, gender isn't arranged on Boy/Girl lines. There are butch women, machos, poofters, lipstick lesbians and drag queens wearing Country Road, and sexual behaviour operates on similarly non-binary lines.

It's a vision of culture which is fundamentally at odds with the conservative demand that we quit messing around with social roles and reaffirm our traditional identities. It's a vision of culture, in fact, which suggests that identities aren't fixed—that gender and sexuality are relational terms, rather than eternal truths. And, in this sense, it's a vision of culture which challenges many of the hierarchies which ground traditional ideas about the family.

The 'family' which lies at the heart of the family values agenda is not a product of nature, it's a creature of ideology. It's a coercive vision of normality. An attempt to impose order, rather than a recognition of the order of things. A set of roles, requirements and rules for relating. As such, it also reveals a strange contradiction in the claim that decent Ordinary Australians have been pushed around lately by weirdos, feminazis and political extremists. In fact, you don't have to look terribly closely at the family values debate to realise that it's the *conservatives* who want to tell the rest of us how to behave.

Opponents of the 'old' political correctness are essentially motivated by the same desire for control. The phrase itself suggests that its opposite must exist—it gestures towards some ideal space outside politics, to a world where everyone already knows their 'correct' place, where politics stays in parliament and women stay at home. To a world where the family and public life are neatly separated and where propertied white men define and run political debate.

Opponents of 'political correctness' are not, as John Howard suggested, in favour of 'free speech'. They're in favour of reinstating some very old rules about who gets to speak, where they do it and what is considered appropriate for public debate. And it's for precisely this reason, that Canberra greeted people like Pauline Hanson into the debate with such astounding silence.

*   *   *

There's no such thing as a free speech. Who gets to speak always depends on who's willing to listen and who's willing to pay for the podium. Like the Greek *agora* which preceded it, the Western public sphere originally defined itself by excluding foreigners, women and the poor. Until this century you needed citizenship, a penis and some property to vote.

Significantly, the Latin word *pubes*, which gave us 'public', means adult male. The conventional idea is that meaningful public debate can only be conducted between reasonable, dispassionate and educated citizens. Everything else is the hysterical catcalling of an unruly mob.

But over the course of the twentieth century the media has radically reshaped our public sphere. What began as a window onto public debate between an elite group has become a frame which defines the debate itself.

Unlike the *agora*, the contemporary public sphere is no longer a physical space—it's virtual. As mass communications scholar, John Hartley, puts it, 'it's graphic rather than geographic'.[9] Public opinion and debate are formed and filtered through the media's lens and, in this sense, the media have come to have a powerful influence not just on who speaks but on how they speak.

Many claim the media—and, in particular, commercial television—corrupt public debate, trivialise the processes of democracy and ignore the claims of marginalised groups. But the recent flurry of conservative panic over everything from feminism to multiculturalism suggests otherwise.

The media's emphasis on lively people, conflict and emotion has opened up a space for a different kind of public speech. Not the reasonable, analytic, highbrow debate of the traditional public sphere—but the impassioned, personal and anecdotal voice of people who've traditionally been expected to shut up and listen.

It's a voice which generally makes the middle class cringe—the voice you hear on talk shows, on talk-back radio and on the myriad current affairs shows which focus on people rather than talking heads. It's a diverse and unruly voice—sometimes it's inflamed with the kind of hatred and fear which animates the likes of Pauline Hanson—but it certainly challenges the idea that the media is a monolithic institution which only talks in the voice of mainstream patriarchy.

The vertiginous spiral of ideas and information we call the mass media isn't a stable platform for pushing political or moral values of any single persuasion. The sheer proliferation of images has eroded the moral authority of any one social order—patriarchal or otherwise. And it's this very collapse which has helped fuel social movements like feminism, Aboriginal land rights and multiculturalism.

Of course, the blokes in suits who are used to running the public sphere aren't terribly impressed with the new, noisy shape of the *agora*. It makes sense that someone like John Howard feels the mere act of having to *listen* to previously voiceless people is some kind of outrageous gag on his own frequently exercised freedom of speech.

Pauline Hanson's claim to the margins is more interesting. Her speech is the kind which propels educated people on the left and the right into an instinctive flinch. Hers *is* a voice most of us don't want to hear. But it's important to distinguish between what she says and what she represents.

Twenty-five years ago, a female fish-and-chip-shop

owner would never have considered running for parliament. Today, as John Howard knows all too well, Hanson's is only one of many new voices laying claim to the public debate.

Pauline Hanson speaks with the strident, faintly self-righteous voice of the excluded. What's more, she believes her own rabid rhetoric. She seriously imagines she's a voice in the wilderness—a whitebread prophet delivering 'real' Australians—Ordinary Australians—from the tyranny of Aboriginals and Asians.

The electoral success of her Us and Them rhetoric raised the question of how Anglo-Australians came to identify, however perversely, with genuinely marginal groups. A partial answer lies in the way groups who were previously seen and not heard, like Aboriginal people, women and the poor, have gained a speaking position in the mass media—a platform which involves something more than letting experts speak for them.

Perversely, Hanson's ability to make herself heard was premised on the breakdown of everything she wants to reinstate—the white, male-dominated public sphere and the 'family values' private domain. A woman with little education, who married in her teens, Hanson remains a potent sign to politicians on both sides of the house that the barbarians are no longer at the gates, they're inside, redecorating the castle in garish new colours.

And this is where Hanson's real political power lies—in her status as a double sign. Her hyperbolic calls for a return to normal 'family' life and a restoration of white privilege are ultimately undercut by the fact that someone of her gender and class is issuing them. Hanson may be calling for an end to 'political correctness' and a return to the old order—but she's a potent symbol that the old political and moral order really is at an end.

Notes

1 Jan Bowen, *Men Talk*, Angus & Robertson, Sydney, 1996.
2 'TV Violence Sickens the Nation', *Sun-Herald*, 20 February 1994, p. 14.
3 Reported in 'The Pope on TV', *Age*, 27 January 1994, p. 11.
4 Reported in 'Hollywood immoral, says Dole', *Sydney Morning Herald*, 13 April 1995, p. 15.
5 'Families in Australia', Australian Institute of Family Studies, Melbourne, 1995.
6 Richard Neville, 'Kill Culture', *The Independent Monthly*, April 1993, pp. 25–27.
7 Senate *Hansard*, 1 March 1995, No. 3, p. 1219.
8 Senate *Hansard*, 1 March 1995, No. 3, p. 1213.
9 J. Hartley, *Popular Reading: Journalism, Modernity, Popular Culture*, Edward Arnold, London, 1996.

Back in the disapproval business

BY DAVID MARR

The jacarandas were nearly over and the Johannesburg streets were a mush of fallen blue flowers. We were picking our way north early one Sunday morning through suburbs turned by slave labour into dream versions of Toorak and Wahroonga. Each innocent garden sat behind its own high wall topped with loops of bougainvillea and razor wire. In my first days in the city I'd wondered why the wire was so naked when so much else was so skilfully hidden. Then I realised. That was the point, these outer defences were meant to be seen as a warning: messy, complicated stuff to engage with, so don't even try.

It was a little before Christmas 1994. The Opposition frontbencher and I had a day to kill in the new South Africa. I'd been up north for the ABC interviewing whores at truckstops on the road to Cairo. He had just flown in from Australia for a conference. We'd made a plan over breakfast to head to Pretoria for the day as tourists. As he drifted in and out of jet lag, I drove north on a beautiful highway, staying hard left to keep out of the path of lethal BMWs speeding to the capital.

At what point we talked about the survey I can't recall, perhaps as we roamed round the Union building—a dud, by the way, a great big Empire dud—and I've only a vague memory of the subject coming up as an ironic counterpoint to the optimism and new freedom of Mandela's South Africa. But what the frontbencher said that day in Pretoria has stuck in my mind: the Liberal Party, a year or so before, had spent a lot of money finding out what would make people in marginal Australian electorates change their vote. They discovered the swinging voter had changed nature: once they were venturesome and forward-looking, now they were deeply cautious particularly in matters of morals. Though these people were not typical Australians of the 1990s, their wish to see old-fashioned values reasserted would be crucial in deciding who next governed Australia. The frontbencher was gloomy personally, but matter-of-fact professionally, about this. And he was sure Labor had done parallel research of its own to reach the same conclusion: swinging voters in Australia wanted government to be seen to be doing something about morals, sex, marriage, drugs and violence—in life and in art.

I remember the day very warmly. We got lost round dusk in a maze of little farms and backroads on the outskirts of Johannesburg. The frontbencher dozed, a big man asleep in a little car. I haven't seen him since. He's now a senior minister in John Howard's cabinet, part of a government being seen to be doing something about films and books and videos and magazines. Indeed, one of the Coalition's few clear-cut policies at the 1996 election was to ban the sale of X-rated videos. This at least they've backed away from. X will now be NVE: non-violent erotica.

Howard was only a few weeks in government when a cool young madman with a passion for powerful guns shot 35 people at Port Arthur. The government banned semi-automatic rifles and announced a ministerial enquiry into the connections between violence on the screen and violence in life. The Minister for Communications and the Arts, Senator Richard Alston, spoke at this time of a 'sea change in community attitudes' to television and video violence. A few days later the Melbourne *Herald Sun* claimed, 'A total of 2000 violent and pornographic videos have been confiscated from the house of alleged Port Arthur mass murderer Martin Bryant ... Many featured violence and explicit sex acts, including bestiality.' This front-page story was nonsense: the videos turned out to be musicals and Hollywood classics. But a 'former girlfriend' told the paper, Bryant's favourite film was *Child's Play 2*, while a man in a video shop cited, instead, Sylvester Stallone's *First Blood*.[1] Whether these films, seen by hundreds of thousands of Australians, played in some criminal way on the young man's imagination was never examined at the government's enquiry or by the court. Indeed, the enquiry reported months before Bryant's trial even began.

The video report in July 1996 was the new government's declaration of support for intensified censorship. Senator Alston recommended a number of complex, showy restrictions on film, video and television: it was time to roll out some razor wire to protect our innocence. He called for V-chips in all new television sets to block transmission of 'violent' material—despite doubts that the technology exists—the recall and reclassification of old videos which might now be considered too violent, the banning of adult movies with levels of violence currently tolerated by the censors and—most eye-catching of all—turning mere *possession* of very violent videos into a criminal offence. None of these measures has yet to become law, but all are still on the table.

Under Paul Keating books and films were already being banned—or in the new terminology 'refused classification'—but the process has picked up speed as the Office of Film and Literature Classification (the Classification Board) responds to the new mood in Canberra under John Howard.

The book called *E is for Ecstasy*, on sale all round the world, is banned in Australia. Seven films on general release in other countries have been banned here by the Classification Board in the past couple of years—though the cult Western *Dead Man* was released after an appeal, and Bruce LaBruce's *Hustler White* was released after cuts. The Spanish art film *Tras es Cristal* (*In a Glass Cage*) was plucked from the official Queerscreen Festival and banned despite protests from the Spanish director, Pedro Almodóvar. Now every film festival in this country faces the prospect of censorship again. Fifty-nine videos have been banned during this time. Parents are solemnly being warned to protect their children from 'The Simpsons'.

The famous spoof Campari ad which *Hustler* magazine fought all the way to the US Supreme Court to publish—a victory celebrated in the film *The People v. Larry Flynt*—was censored in the Australian edition of the magazine by the Classification Board. The word 'mom' was blacked out six times to remove a suggestion of incest. Meanwhile, Richard Alston has urged the ABC to consider seriously the complaints of 60 people who don't want to watch the Sydney Mardi Gras on television. Six hundred and fifty thousand people packed the streets to see the parade in 1996 and 1.2 million saw it on television, but the minister called those 60 complaints 'a significant level of community concern'.[2]

The fearful have never ceased calling for censorship. What began to happen under Labor, and now more strongly under the Coalition, is that politicians—for reasons both complex and simple—are *listening* to those voices again. Sheer whingeing has played its part in wearing the politicians down. The power of persistent complaint should never be overlooked in public life. Even groundless complaints have to be faced and dealt with. All over Australia, politicians are not only fearful of the way the tide is running, but rather tired. They are giving in, hoping to still those narking voices that have never stopped over the last 25 apparently libertarian years—but they're probably heading for the mire. All the experience of the past suggests that once governments begin to give in to calls for censorship—once they get back into the disapproval business—the pressure for censorship builds.

Canberra seems to have forgotten what it was like in the late 1960s when we were the Ireland of the South Pacific. Government was then caught in the vice-like logic of its role: so active were police and customs officers at banning and culling—all the works of Henry Miller, pot-boilers like *The Carpetbaggers*, D. H. Lawrence's *Lady Chatterley's Lover*, Norman Mailer's anti-war tract *Why Are We In Vietnam?*, etc. etc.—that anything *not* censored seemed to come with a stamp of approval from Canberra. To dispel this politically embarrassing impression, even more thorough censorship was undertaken ...

How all this changed is a story that's often been told. I had a tiny bit part in the process. In my very brief legal career, I was the dogsbody on the team that was defending Philip Roth's novel *Portnoy's Complaint*, that little master-piece of masturbation which first federal customs and then the state police declared obscene in 1970. Courts backed the police all round Australia except in Sydney where two juries refused to convict the novel. Those two hung juries did the trick. We don't know who the jurors were; and we have no idea if those men and women fairly represented the Australian community; but they ended book censorship in Australia.

Crucial to the liberalisation that followed—under the last Liberal governments of that era and then under Gough Whitlam—was the death of the tiny, Catholic, conservative breakaway Democratic Labor Party, which had used its often crucial position in the Senate to hold the line on censorship. The DLP was a one-truth party, passionately anti-communist, with little respect for other dissenting voices—inside or outside politics. It took for granted the moral obligation of the State to censor books and films. Government had the power and government must use the power. Of course, the belief that police and customs offi-cers should be directed to do the work of God extended far beyond the Catholic church, indeed beyond organised religion. It has never gone away.

Essentially what has happened now, is that that const-ituency has won back the strategic leverage lost in the early 1970s. They are the swinging voters of today, the heirs of the DLP. Their man in Parliament is Brian Harradine, who sits on the Senate Committee on Community Standards, one of the oddest organs in the Australian body politic.

*   *   *

Hunched on the red benches like a grasshopper in a grey suit, Harradine is alert to every strategic possibility in the parliamentary air. At times his slate-blue eyes dart about the chamber before returning to a steady, rather hard focus. His brow furrows and his upper lip has a way of closing like a tiny prehensile beak. He never loses his temper. In the Senate he displays three exceptional qualities which have marked his long career: persuasion, persistence and grasp of the rules—whether they are the rules of the unions he led early on in Tasmania, or the rules of the Senate, or the rules of his church as set out in Paul VI's *Humanae Vitae* to which he is devoted.

Brian Harradine is now the father of the Senate and the longest-surviving independent in the history of the Australian parliament. Since Paul Keating's re-election in 1993, he has held the balance of power in the upper house: in the face of a combined Opposition, no government can pass legislation without his support. He is a walking veto. And with John Howard's election, the senator has found a government more willing than any in the past two decades to deliver him what he wants.

Though his principal interest is gynaecological—he wants no Medicare payments for abortions and IVF, an end to government support for family planning in Australia and birth control programs in the Third World, etc.—censorship is high on Harradine's list. He is committed to tougher controls on sex and violence in film and television, and to seeing controls extended to each new medium as it reaches Australia: video games, fantasy phone lines, pay television, and the Internet.

Yet he remains extremely reluctant to address the philosophical—largely doctrinal—basis of all this. 'If you want to know what I believe,' he says, 'just go back through *Hansard*.'[3] There you find a rather scrappy record, for Harradine works in Parliament by clever intervention, not expressions of belief. Over the years, he has complained, among other things, about university radio stations, feminists on government boards, women's counselling services, AIDS advertising on Father's Day, the employment of communists by Amnesty International, lesbian access to IVF, retrospective tax legislation, homosexual partners being treated as spouses, ditto de factos, any experiments on any embryo— 'this most vulnerable human life.'[4]—degradation of women in sex videos, phone sex, laws protecting lesbians and homosexuals from discrimination at work, ultrasound machines, and the World Bank.

At the core of all this, and deeper perhaps than his Catholic faith, is a heartfelt wish that life be simple. It is here that Harradine strikes a chord with the newly fearful swinging voters of marginal Australia: a wish to go back to what seem, in memory, better times when families held together and we all had jobs, when friends and foes were easily identified in the world, when television didn't have the gritty flavour of today and children were safe from whatever dangers lurked in videos and video games because those weren't even invented then. Even in retrospect we know it was not an entirely innocent world, but looking back it seems that in those times evil influences were at least combatable.

Harradine was always a combatant. He came from a Catholic Labor family. His grandfather, two uncles and three of his brothers were all in the trade union movement. At first he heard the call of the church, but left the seminary after a couple of years and became an organiser for the Clerks Union. This was in South Australia where Labor had split in the great factional brawls of the early 1950s. Harradine was briefly a member of the DLP but resigned before heading to Hobart at the age of 24 to organise the union. Labor had not split in Tasmania and Harradine joined the party in 1961. By the end of the decade he was secretary of Hobart Trades Hall, a member of the ACTU executive, and was about to take his seat on the Federal Executive of the Labor Party when he issued his famous claim that 'friends of Communists' would prevent him.

So the Harradine Affair began. For the man it was a crusade. For the Left, it was a brawl to consolidate the numbers. For the Labor Party, the Affair was immensely damaging, all its dreary, complex length. Harradine was finally expelled from the party in 1975. It's said the Russian parliament was discussing the liturgy of the Orthodox Church when the Revolution struck. Labor, as it plunged towards the Sacking, was debating Brian Harradine. He found himself free in December to stand for the Senate as an independent and, in a poll which all but annihilated Labor in Tasmania, Harradine was elected. He has held his place in the Senate ever since with a core support of about 11 per cent of his state. Harradine speaks with the voice of only about 32,000 Tasmanians—but what matters is not his backing but his Senate vote.

No great debate marked the creation of his Senate Select Committee on Community Standards Relevant to the Supply of Services Utilising Electronic Technologies—known as the Standards or sometimes the Morals Committee—which grew out of earlier Senate enquiries into the X-rated video industry, enquiries in which Harradine had also been deeply involved. (X allows explicit sex between adults and mild non-violent fetishes, but no sexual violence of any kind.) The old committee wanted an end to X. The new Standards Committee then began life in 1991 investigating fantasy phone services but then took root and flourished. There Labor pooled the most persistent Senate whingers about sex and vice and violence in film, television and video. Feminist concerns were represented too, and so were true liberals of both major parties. But the overall mood of the committee has been deeply conservative and members report intractable meetings with little common ground between the advocates and opponents of censorship. The liberals tend to fall away, exhausted, while the conservatives sit tight: two who have survived from the start are John Tierney and Brian Harradine.

The crucial senator believes sex in films and video degrades women, misleads men into thinking women are 'available', and generally promotes promiscuity. Hence AIDs. He assumes without question that violence inspires violence. His rhetoric rests on the needs of children—entirely innocent, malleable: blank books for evil's pen—but argues adults need protecting too. 'Censorship is the application of a carefully balanced and judiciously evaluated assessment of that which is conducive to the essential common good of an equal, free and life-affirming society.'[5] A very wide range of material is not, in his judgement, conducive to such a society—starting with X-rated videos.

Essential to Harradine's position—and to the arguments of his allies inside and outside the Senate—is the notion that all this is somehow new. Harradine attacks the Labor Party's official policies because they 'arose out of the debates 20 years ago that some saw as a battle between the literati and the philistines over the survival of both new and old writings.'[6] His colleague on the committee, Margaret Reynolds, asserts that this 'is no longer the old censorship debate of the 1960s'.[7]

But only the rhetoric has changed—rhetoric and the ways film and writing reach their destination. There was no video, pay TV, no Internet back then. And one of the oldest traditions of this sad business, a tradition going back beyond Gutenburg, is to see the new as especially potent. So the invention of each 'delivery system'—from type to bytes—means a fresh and more urgent need to censor.

The first big victory for the Community Standards Committee was to block R-rated films for pay television. Such films are standard fare on pay television around the world and research—somewhat ambiguous—commissioned by the committee showed 82 per cent of Australians were happy with the idea of R on pay. But this result the committee could not accept, for the demonisation of R is an essential tactic in the new push for censorship.

Yet R is not porn, nor is R extremely violent. Films thought too violent are—often ludicrously—cut or 'refused classification' in Australia. R allows sex 'realistically implied or simulated' and violence that is 'highly realistic' but 'not unduly detailed, relished or cruel'.[8] R films like *Trainspotting*, *Postcards from America*, and *What I Have Written* are thought suitable by the Classification Board to be seen by anyone over 17 in a cinema but will not now be screened on general pay channels. That astonishing decision was made, at the instigation of the committee, by Labor.

Now under the Coalition, the Senate committee is listened to as never before. As a guide to what lies ahead for this country, the most important development is the Howard government's endorsement of the committee's old complaint that the men and women who work for the Classification Board somehow don't represent the real Australia. Senator Alston joined this attack, calling 'too many' of the Board's censors 'experts or so-called professionals' who become cynical and 'desensitised' to violence after years of seeing films. Parents, he suggested, would do a better job. 'They are more likely to give you a direct response from the heartland of Australia.'[9]

Yet the Office of Film and Literature Classification is required by law to reflect community standards in its decisions. Overseeing its work are the 'censoring ministers'— usually the attorneys-general of the states, territories and Commonwealth. All are politicians representing their electorates, their parties and their governments. The present batch might, according to *Who's Who* and other sources, be described as a bunch of football-loving lawyers who read a bit and rarely watch films. The ministers in turn approve the appointment of the officers who actually do the work of classifying films, videos, books and magazines. These 18 men and women represent the community in their own way. At the moment they include teachers, community workers, a dairy farmer, ex-journalists, an Asian film buff, psychologists, a psychiatrist, child-care workers, a Catholic priest, and television news presenter Anne Fulwood. Between them they have lots of degrees, lots of children, and live in a politically useful pattern across the continent. Running the office is a seasoned bureaucrat, once a ministerial press secretary, who has proved a deft survivor for over 20 years in the shifting political allegiances of Canberra. He's a man who can sniff the wind. Indeed, already the Classification Board under his direction has banned and cut enough films and videos to cause alarm among those who fear a return to the old days of censorship in Australia. Under pressure, the Classification Board in 1996 issued new consolidated guidelines that mean tougher restrictions on screen violence, restrictions which were widely deplored by the film industry.

Despite this cautious drift the Community Standards Committee believes the Classification Board is radically libertarian and does not represent the true Australian community. Nor, according to the Senate committee, do the in-house censors of the commercial television stations and the regulators of the Australian Broadcasting Tribunal. That all three report very low levels of public complaint about their work does not sway the committee from its view that all these regulatory bodies are out of touch with Australia.

For some time Harradine's committee has been advocating that citizens' panels should be established to review decisions of the Office of Film and Literature Classification. These panels would represent 'major interest groups such as parents, teachers, churches, academics, women, youth, aboriginal and ethnic representatives'. Senator Alston was alluding to this notion when he spoke of bringing representatives of the 'heartland' into the censorship business. Even so, this idea of a parallel system of citizen censors was treated rather as a joke round Canberra until the Howard government suddenly announced a few days after Christmas 1996 that it accepted the core of the committee's plan. The Federal Attorney-General spoke of the panels working as 'auditors' of the Classification Board's work—but without the power to overturn them. The censoring ministers decided in March 1997 to set up the first 'Community Assessment Panels' in Sydney but left still undecided most of the crucial questions:

what weight has to be given to these citizens' opinions? Could the board afford to ignore them altogether? What happens if a gulf opens up between the two sets of decisions? Which films, videos, books, magazines and computer games are they going to be shown? All of them? A sample at random? Who will the governments of the states, territories and Commonwealth trust to choose the panels? And, above all, where will these true representatives of the Australian community be found? Perhaps among the swinging voters in marginal electorates across the continent.

*   *   *

Hustler White drew a modest crowd to its Australian opening in a Sydney art house cinema off Oxford Street in March 1997. What we saw at the Chauvel that night was no masterpiece. Nor was it the film on general release in the United States, Germany and New Zealand. Cuts had been made on the orders of the Classification Board. The distributors, pressed for time and cash, had not put up a fight.

Prosecutions and trials were once what alerted us to censorship in Australia. Not now. The fight has gone out of the trade. The ordinary reality today is that no one is fighting censorship in the courts. No one is defying authority as Penguin Books did when they published that Australian edition of *Portnoy* and invited prosecution. The American publishers of *Hustler* went to court for the right to mock the preacher Jerry Falwell in that spoof Campari ad, but in Australia the magazine accepted the Classification Board's direction that it mustn't mention 'mom'.

'Jurgen, a writer, comes to LA to write a book about gay hustling. Jurgen falls in love with a hit and run driver, a hustler called Monty. Together they explore the hustling scene.' So begins the Classification Board's report on *Hustler White*. The distributor, Mark Spratt, had already cut a few seconds showing an erect penis and blacked out three or four moments of what he feared the Board might take to be actual sex. Those cuts were not enough.

'At 26 minutes,' said the report, 'an older male client stands fully naked, his hands chained to the ceiling. A male hustler implicitly burns him several times with a lit cigarette. The client says, "Delicious, dear boy". There are very discreet visuals of burn marks. At 27 minutes the hustler draws a razor blade embedded in a thin strip of wood across the client's body leaving bloody cuts across his back and buttocks. The cutting is filmed in close-up. The scene is entirely consensual as the client encourages the hustler saying, "Cut my buttocks, dear boy". A medium shot shows the man's very bloody back and buttocks criss-crossed with lacerations.'

A minority of the board thought the scene 'could be accommodated in the R classification as it occurs in a film of considerable merit and would be likely to find strong acceptance amongst audiences interested in Queer culture.' But they were outvoted by the majority who thought the razor blade scene 'an offensive depiction of sexual activity accompanied by fetishes, or practices which are offensive or abhorrent and which warrants an RC classification (Refused Classification). The theme of mutilation for pleasure is one which has a high degree of intensity and the treatment is very detailed with repeated close-up visuals of the cuts being made and dribbling blood.'

Sitting there in the Chauvel, it was hard to take seriously the censors' moral distinction between slashing and

burning. And the impossibly funny result is that by ordering cuts to those few seconds of slashing, the Classification
Board has, in effect, endorsed burning a bound man with
a blazing cigarette butt as an *acceptable* fetish. Will the
Attorney-General stand in Parliament and defend this
exquisite distinction?

Mark Spratt resubmitted the film with fresh cuts and
it was classified R. 'You could have got that scene through
almost any time in the last 20 years,' said Spratt. 'Films in
the seventies did that and they were an R. There are lots
of films out there that would not be passed today. They
were tolerant then.'[10] While the government works to
undermine a supposedly radical and out-of-touch Classifi-
cations Board, Spratt is one of those within the film industry railing against the caution its decisions are already
revealing. And he is also at loggerheads with those who
argue the censors have become desensitised by years on the
job. On the contrary: 'it's as if they've never seen a film.'[11]

The Classification Board is moving deep into the disapproval business. Consent is a key worry of the Board
these days and also a difficulty with *Hustler White*. 'Another
scene between 50 and 57 minutes shows a hustler engaging
in simulated sexual activity with a number of large, mostly
black men . . . the scene is humourously established as consensual after all the men stop in their activity to answer
pagers. The hustler calls out "Next!" after taking his call.
However, prior to that, visuals of sexual activity are very
strongly implied and consent is uncertain. At the end of
the scene a man says to the naked hustler, "So you think
you were raped . . . it was merely an exercise in black-
power." The lengthy scene is intercut with Jurgen and
Monty talking and hustling. A majority of the Board felt

that this scene could be accommodated at the R level as consent is established and violence does not take place. A minority of the Board felt that consent was not clearly and consistently established and that the accompanying atmosphere of threat or menace in this lengthy scene makes it sufficiently offensive to warrant RC classification.'

Mark Spratt said: 'It's a film for adults.'[12]

Would it have made a difference if *Hustler White* were a work of art? Perhaps. But in the new mood of censorship, art has all but lost its voice. When poor sick Portnoy was in the dock 25 years ago, art was a defence to charges of obscenity. Not always and not in every state, but under the law of New South Wales and Victoria an obscene book could still be published if it had high literary merit. Art was the key. The defence of art went back to the origins of laws against obscenity in England, which, originally, were only meant to apply to trash. But under the 1995 legislation setting up the Office of Film and Literature Classification, art is no longer a defence. Art has been downgraded to a consideration, one of the 'matters' to be taken into account in classifying books and films, magazines and video games.

Whose judgement matters here? At least while the current system lasts, the ultimate judgement is that of the censoring ministers who meet three times a year to fine-tune the board's classification guidelines. The discussions of the ministers are detailed and often heated. They argue about individual books and watch uncut films—like Disney's *The Rock*—to debate their classification. They work by consensus, which in the politics of this country gives an advantage to the cautious and conservative. But at last count, the nine ministers didn't include a real film buff. One likes theatre, three list music among their recreations,

and four like to read. But by far and away their most pas-
sionate recreation is football. In *Who's Who*, Denver Bean-
land, Attorney-General of Queensland, cites all four codes:
rules, league, union and soccer.

The censoring ministers approved a set of detailed
guidelines for classification of film and video in July 1995.
Although the Act clearly says that artistic merit is to be
taken into account, there is nothing in the guidelines to
show what bearing artistic questions have on the process
of film and video classification. Art is not the key. Some
respect for cinematic values remains among the censors
themselves. When the Classification Board upheld the
10-year ban on Passolini's *Salo*, the Review Board, an in-
house court of appeal, decided to allow public screening
with an R certificate because of *Salo*'s cinematic merit. That
decision is, perhaps, the single greatest source of complaint
against the board by pro-censorship forces in the
community.

Art's standing is as shaky now in the world of books.
Again, the legislation says literary merit has to be considered when censoring books but the regulations say nothing
to guide the censor's assessment of literary merit as they
ponder which publications must never be imported or published in Australia, and which can be sold—wrapped or
unwrapped in cellophane. If art comes into the question,
it's only by courtesy of the civilised instincts of the censors.
They talk at the board of 'bona fide' authors and the need
to take a more liberal view of those writers' work. But there
is, alas, no trace now of the old understanding that books
which might otherwise fall foul of the censor may be
redeemed entirely by their merit as art.

So far, the most dramatic recent book banning has

involved drugs not art. *E is for Ecstasy* is on sale all round the world but banned in Australia. Why? Because the new classification rules are riddled with the rhetoric of the War against Drugs. This is bizarre; R-rated movies may show violence, simulated sex and rough language but are not allowed to give 'detailed instruction to drug misuse'. X-rated videos allow adults to thrash about enjoying real sex but must not depict drug addiction if it offends against 'the standards of morality, decency and general propriety generally accepted by reasonable adults'.

The pleasures of ecstasy are a particular political worry in the 1990s. Bob Carr had not seen Baz Luhrmann's *Romeo and Juliet* when he ventured that his Department of School Education should be encouraged to screen the film and so begin a Luhrmann-led recovery of 'serious literature'—but only after cutting details of Romeo taking ecstacy. Luhrmann standing by the Premier's side might have argued his film illustrates the very unhappy outcome of making romantic commitments while on the drug. Instead he simply refused to countenance a cut. 'Look, in one country they wanted to cut the kiss. And guess what? I wouldn't let them. The film is complete.'[13]

*   *   *

Absurdity always goes with this territory—and ridicule has always been the best weapon of those who want to make up their own minds about the books they write and read, the films they make and see. The fight has always, in a sense, been between conservative whingeing and libertarian ridicule. Laughter buried the puritans last time: by the early 1970s censorship had become, essentially, a joke. There's lots of fresh comedy about now. As this book was going to press the Community Standards Committee issued another batch of recommendations. Not all are foolish, but they include pasting labels on R-rated videos to warn they may harm depressives, taking the word 'suicide' out of pop songs and banning all 'disturbing footage' from the early evening television news.

Less amusing are calls to take censorship into new territory: Australia's video stores. At present the general rule is that a film goes from cinema to video with the same classification: M remains M, and what's R at a Hoyts multiplex is R in the video store. Tough penalties already apply to shops caught renting videos to anyone underage. But the Standards Committee wants videos cut, reclassified and in some cases banned, in the belief that watching a video is somehow more dangerous than sitting in the cinema watching a film, for you can see the violent bits again and again and again.

Laughter here must be mixed with pity. No absolute connection has ever been established between violent videos—or films, or books, or magazines, or video games, or comics—and violent behaviour. The most violent films come out of the most orderly society on earth: Japan. There is no end of true and awful accounts of violent people watching violent videos. But to ignore all other factors—all kinds of misery and frustration, poverty and alcohol—and treat videos as the cause of their violence requires a persistent act of faith.

Perhaps the most reasonable way of making sense of our appetite for censorship is to see it, finally, as an act of faith—of Christian faith. Proponents may conscript any useful argument to bolster their campaign—the dignity of women, the health hazards of heroin, the dangers of rape—

but evidence that censorship achieves any of these ends is not considered vital. Why? Because at heart this is not a matter of logic but obligation. The true purpose of censorship, even if barely acknowledged, is to fulfil the Christian duty of shielding the frail from temptation. And in the light of faith, we are all frail ...

Here we are back to fundamentals. What might otherwise be dismissed as a joke now makes sense. At stake here is the prospect of everlasting life. No wonder the whingers are so persistent. No wonder the churches have always been a powerhouse for censorship. No wonder governments let themselves be persuaded into the disapproval business.

The faithful are unmoved by coarse, secular arguments that censorship doesn't work. So much is at stake, they say, that we must *try* even if the printing press and the video recorder and the Internet make censorship all but impossible. But who of us even needs Portnoy to learn how to masturbate or heavy metal to plant the idea of committing suicide? Our bodies give us most of what we need to know about sex, and what our bodies don't tell us we pick up in the playground. The history of censorship is a history of failure.

But Canberra, still setting up shop in the censorship business, isn't considering how it will all end. Like last time—and those of us who go back that little way, should remind Australia what it was like then, when Canberra was so heavily engaged in the disapproval business it all but lost the power to say no.

(Much of this material appeared in different form in the *Sydney Morning Herald* in 1996 and 1997.)

Notes

1 *Herald Sun*, 14 May 1996, p. 1.
2 *Sydney Morning Herald*, 5 November 1996, p. 3.
3 Harradine to Marr, interview, 17 January 1997.
4 Senate *Hansard*, 23 April 1985, Vol. S. 108, p. 1396.
5 *Sydney Morning Herald*, 9 January 1989, p. 9.
6 ibid.
7 Senate *Hansard*, 28 June 1995, Vol. S. 172, p. 2005.
8 Office of Film and Literature Classification, Guidelines for the Classification of Films and Videos.
9 *Sydney Morning Herald*, 10 July 1996, p. 1.
10 Spratt to Marr, interview, 19 February 1997.
11 ibid.
12 ibid.
13 *Sydney Morning Herald*, 1 February 1997, p. 4.

Sticks and stones and stereotypes: what are 'speech codes' for?

BY MEAGHAN MORRIS

Every time someone learns to chant that 'sticks and stones may break my bones, but names can never hurt me', a lesson is passed on about language. Several lessons, really. We learn, first of all, to tell a whopping lie about language—and usually, about ourselves. Names can hurt all right, even if they don't break bones; as children, we learn to say they can't precisely because they just have ('There, there, don't cry: remember, "Sticks and stones ..."'). Names hurt hearts and minds and souls, and a 'me' truly *never* hurt by names would be utterly impervious to all other human beings—an angel or a sociopath, perhaps.

Yet the lesson of the chant is not itself a lie, but a magical theory of language: 'saying makes it so'. The chant is an incantation, a spell that we cast at aggressors to keep the power of their words at bay. When someone pelts words at us to try to hurt our feelings, we block them with a ritual formula that vows they will never succeed. So, like all good spells, this formula 'means' something different from what it seems to say: 'names can never hurt me' means '*you* can't hurt me—who cares what you think? *Your* insults are powerless; you don't matter, and I am stronger than you are.'

We may be telling the truth or we may be dying inside. Either way, the chant teaches us an art of self-defence along with some basic facts of social life. We learn that language is powerful, and we can do things to each other with words; that language is a social bond, as flexible as it is forceful; and that meaning depends on how we *use* language in all the varying situations of life. From its singsong cadence, we also learn something obvious that language-moralists forget when they call some words good and others irredeemably bad: there's a lot more to language than names— or verbs and prepositions, for that matter. The powers of language, written or spoken, include rhythm, tone, accent, pitch, and rhyme as well as reason. How something is said affects us as much as who says it and why: we may accept an 'affectionate insult' from a friend more easily than from a stranger, but if the friend says the same thing in a nasty tone in the middle of an argument, affectionate words become stinging. Much more than a way of describing things and trading information, language is a relationship between people. However routine or perfunctory most everyday contact may be, we touch each other with words.

Some verbal gestures pack a wallop no magic spell can contain. I learned this one morning in about 1965, when I walked to school like every other day, past the cow paddock and the shops, under the railway bridge and past the prison farm, then up the road dividing the brick of Maitland Girls' High School from the stone of Maitland Gaol. Since I did this every day, I hardly ever watched where I was going; sleepy from reading into the night and doing homework before breakfast, I floated, snoozed and chatted myself to school. On that particular morning, from half-way up the hill even I could see through my dreamy haze the white letters on the dull brick wall:

MEAGHAN MORRIS IS A SLUT

They seemed to be enormous, sky-high. And so bright! As the world froze quietly inside me, I wondered if people could see my name from the main street miles away. No doubt at all, every pupil and teacher could; girls were hanging off the fence by their fingernails to see what I would do.

'Stereotypes ... take away a person's individuality', says *Language Matters*, a brochure for staff and students at the University of Technology, Sydney. They certainly do: with a glancing gesture—'spastic', 'wog', 'dole-bludger', 'dwarf', 'slant-eyes', 'slut', 'dirty-boong' (there are hundreds of ways to do this)—a human personality is squashed into someone else's idea of its essential shape in less than a second flat. Hurled at people as insults or whispered around them as rumours, stereotypes are also intensely isolating. From a comfortable, warm, hissing little place secured for 'all of *us*' we turf out *them*, the scapegoats—the ones publicly punished for breaking the rules so the rest of us know what they are.

It's quite a spectacle. Luckily, I knew what a scapegoat should do to survive the next five minutes: keep walking, look at nothing, eyeball anyone who stood in my way; push through, scrape an ankle or two if necessary, go inside, open a book. I'd been bullied by experts as a child in a small rural town; 'four-eyes!', 'commie!' and 'swot!' were the names I feared then, for the pinching and punching that followed. When someone ground my face into a wall as a short-cut to breaking my glasses, my father taught me how to fight back. The effect was astonishing: after months of muttering about sticks and stones, I flattened one of my tormentors once and it stopped. Still, I'd been happy to move to Maitland, a cosmopolitan city where quite a few kids wore glasses and had politically incorrect parents who didn't like Mister Menzies.

Verbally humiliated in my new home, I should have been shattered but I wasn't. Maybe all that chanting toughened me up. At any rate, the wall was slinging the wrong name at the wrong 14-year-old virgin. Far from being a slut, I was still a swot. The message should have read (in the idiom of those halcyon days of Australian cultural unity), MEAGHAN MORRIS READS DIRTY BOOKS. My downfall was a book by Bertrand Russell, probably *Why I Am Not a Christian*. I found it in the town library and it shocked me to the core: what if people could live good lives without going to church? What if I tried to think for myself what the right way to live might be? What if you could love someone without getting married?

Reading didn't make me a slut. Talking about it did. On the bus, I told a boy I knew slightly about this amazing book I was reading. Not a total fool, I confided in him only because I thought he was like me, 'bookish'—picked on, I'd heard, by the boys at school. In the solitude of my second five minutes as a scapegoat, I understood he'd sold me out to buy in with those boys. I couldn't really blame him. Besides, 'slut' was a step up from 'swot' if both were just rude names for reading—a warmer, more friendly social identity. I hitched up my uniform, grew my hair, and never looked back.

Because we touch each other with words, language passes on values: yes, no, good, bad, maybe, so-so . . . what if? The writing on that wall spelt out the 'codes' of language and my community in mid-1960s Australia. It told me that ideas were dangerous when merely to ask 'what if?' could put you beyond the pale; that thinking freely was a sin and speaking openly a vice; that conformity was valued more than truth. It also told me, 'it's different for girls': a boy-swot might have been called a 'poof' instead of a slut, but no boy would have been punished by his peers for contemplating sex outside marriage—unless (unthinkably in those days) he declared *himself* a poof. So it told me my egalitarian society had rigid, intolerant rules of speech that assured my inequality.

'PC language': the boot on the other's foot?

Most people can tell a story about facing up to insults, abuse, unpopularity or even persecution at some point in their lives. Whether told as funny anecdotes, painful confessions, or 'life-is-hard-get-used-to-it' moral fables, whether recounting trivial incidents or one person's experience of mass suffering and oppression, these stories are important to those who tell them. They help us explain who we are and how we feel about others in the present.

They are not much help in understanding the fuss about so-called 'politically correct' language that has broken out over the past few years. They don't explain why 'speech codes' have suddenly appeared in workplaces, public organisations, and universities—supposedly bastions of free speech—or what these codes have to do with censorship, anti-vilification laws, defamation and protests about advertisements. At best, tales of tough times survived in closed, intolerant little communities may have an indirect bearing on debates about what counts as civil behaviour in big, diverse social spaces densely populated by strangers—and open to the world.

True, after all the hysteria and myth-mongering of recent years about the 'enforcement' of 'PC' language in Australian institutions, it's useful to remember just how strictly speech was policed back in the good old days when minorities weren't noisy, and how effectively name-calling, stereotyping, shunning and moral pressure kept women, wogs and weirdos in their place. These, the modern methods of imposing orthodoxy without breaking bones, were not invented in the 1980s by academic leftists and their media mates, and they certainly have not vanished with the election of John Howard.

There is always orthodoxy in human affairs, and someone who loves to impose it. For people puzzled by an abrasive new sensitivity to words in social life, or stung by a hostile reaction to their harmless comment as 'sexist' or 'racist', it is plausible as well as comforting to believe there is nothing new in all this—just another rabid bunch of bullies telling ordinary people how to talk. The fuss is blamed on former scapegoats, exacting revenge for real or imagined slights in the past—the boot on the other's foot.

It happens. But it would be wrong to suggest that nothing changes under the sun but the scapegoats in season—wogs and weirdos a while ago, rednecks and Anglo-Celts yesterday, 'feminazis' and 'the Aboriginal industry' today. Shifts in language are actually related to deep social change. Even 'orthodoxy' isn't what it used to be in Christian-dominated societies. Once it was the name of a state to which almost everyone sane aspired. Now, 'orthodoxy' is a term of abuse for *other* people's beliefs, and those who want to influence public opinion routinely pose as heretics—often in the name of 'the silent majority'. It is rare in Australia to hear someone say, '*I* am orthodox . . .'. *They* are orthodox, and minor, and in the wrong; *we* are heretical, mainstream, and right.

All this overblown rhetoric obscures the fact that most of the time in modern democracies we are comparing different orthodoxies and assessing their implications. Faced with rival models of how we ought to act—say, one that relentlessly stomps on every single expression of social prejudice, or one that bellows 'I can call your kid a mongrel if I want to, so you shut up about it!'—the practical issue before us has nothing to do with 'correctness' in the sense of conformity to an orthodoxy. It is which of these codes of behaviour is more likely to shape a tolerant society that cherishes debate, protects dissent, and gives us all a chance to participate.

If I had to choose between these extremes, I'd take my chances with the first one. Po-faced puritanism is usually too busy finding sins and crimes within (more sexism and racism, just where you'd least expect it!) to organise social violence against scapegoats or outsiders. But the main thing wrong with the notion that PC is just a new brand of intolerance is that it fools us into thinking that we do, as a community, face choices of such stark simplicity, that today's battles about language are just like yesterday's wars of ideology, and that the world hasn't changed in 30 years.

PC sympathisers indulge this fantasy too when they laugh at people's anxieties that speech matters in strange new ways, or their fears that any casual utterance might expose them to criticism.

It can happen—why deny it? We all see it on television every other week. When Queensland National Party MP Bob Katter mixed up 'slanty' and 'squinty' in an unloving ode to feminazi eyes, all hell broke loose in the media. Paul Keating caused an international incident when he called the Malaysian Prime Minister, Dr Mahathir, recalcitrant instead of intransigent. Watching the feeding frenzy that follows whenever somebody trips on their tongue, it's not surprising if everyone who has ever mixed up a few words wonders when their turn will come.

Language does have a new kind of volatility in Australian social and economic life. I remember when words were used sparsely: men said little when they came home from work, women did family business at morning tea, and no-one talked politics or religion at dinner (for good reason, in a society where 'mixed marriages' were Catholic–Protestant and families were wrecked by sectarianism). 'PC language' is an issue in a different world. Today, words, symbols, images, interpersonal gestures, the relationships they create and the feelings they provoke are the very stuff of the service and culture industries, in which carelessly giving offence is bad business practice and employment is insecure. A working day has no definite end for those who work, and word-machines fill the home; few women now can care full-time for families alone, and politicial, religious, social and, yes, linguistic disputes stream off the TV over breakfast, lunch and dinner.

At the same time, new communications technologies

and the expansion of education and tourism have, quite as powerfully as immigration and multiculturalism, increased our exposure to other people's parochialisms and to ideas of civility that differ from our own. The noise of all this difference can no more be kept out of Australian social spaces than words can be stripped of their social power. In this world, the truly 'excommunicated' are not professional heretics fighting this or that 'correct line', but people left without access to jobs, education and technology; those without word-machines and 'pc' (personal computer) skills are beginning to be excluded from society. If promoters of unpopular ideas do suffer for their faith, they can tell the world about it; new media are giving the most eccentric people ways to find partners in dissent.

Public institutions are changing along with the rest of society. Once, universities were communities of people like-minded enough to stage a few ding-dong battles that made sense to everyone. The Sydney University I attended in the 1970s was more homogeneous than a country town with a bit of a woman shortage. It didn't always seem so at the time; coming from Maitland, I spent two years of what I thought was culture shock with aliens from North Shore Sydney. However, most students I met were Australian-born, about the same age, white, Christian or lapsed, studied full-time, had middle-class backgrounds or, like me, aspirations, and spoke English as a first or fluent second language.

Today, someone entering a classroom in all but a few elite institutions can take none of these things for granted, not one—except for, usually, the middle-class aspirations. Universities now are not communal *at all*. They are huge networks—or networks of networks, if the truth be told—of communities linked to other communities inside and outside the university, the city, the state, and the nation. They are diverse in composition from the outset, without anyone needing to 'impose' multiculturalism, and they vary from each other.

These changes have practical consequences that are only slowly filtering through to public debate. In the 1970s, it was meaningful to talk of 'academics' and 'students' as social groups with coherent fashion tendencies in ideas as well as clothing: the cartoon image of the typical PC activist as a spiky-haired, be-overalled, jack-booted feminist belongs to that era, along with the tweedy professor. There are people who match both images. However, as tenure declines, short-term contracts become normal, and teachers come in from industry, community groups and foreign countries to perform specific tasks, the academic body is becoming as diverse and fluid as the student body is at any given time.

Universities are not the only institutions discussed in a language or a set of stereotypes that no longer help us deal with reality. There is a reality-lag between the economic and social changes of the past 30 years and how we represent them, which makes it hard to imagine their consequences. Thus some people dream of reviving the family values of the 1950s and 1960s, while embracing the destruction of the protected, unionised, job-for-life, full white male employment, eight-hour-day economy which sustained them. In language matters, reality-lag inclines us to go on talking *about* 'language' as though it were a single issue, something part of but detachable from the rest of our social lives—a tool to use, but sparely.

The idea that there is a coherent 'politically correct language' movement—a visible group of people who stomp on every expression of what they see as prejudice—is a product of this lag. It isn't a myth in the sense of having no basis in reality. It is a stereotype that makes it harder to deal with reality. There are many conflicts about language use in societies which are open and diverse (sometimes more so than we are prepared to deal with or accept), and different people have varying views about all of them. This student is insulted by racial epithets while believing on religious grounds that homosexuality is evil. That student loathes white feminists. This one jumps on every second word that other people say, while being tone-deaf to the meanings of rural or working-class speech. That one couldn't care less about words and wants to get on with finding a job.

By the same token, the same person can oppose the passing of laws against vilification (as I do, thinking that it does more harm than good), while supporting the minimal censorship of books and films we had in Australia until recently; attack racist cartoons selling beer or washing machines, without wanting to have them banned; oppose campaigns against gorgeous bodies on billboards; and think it a good idea for workplaces to offer guidelines to polite, fair and realistic ways of talking to a mixed bunch of strangers. These issues have not been created by PC militants. They arise from practical problems of daily life in diverse, democratic societies, and neither mockery nor stereotyping will make them go away.

Courtesy or euphemism: what are speech codes for?

In a very funny film called *Demolition Man*, Sylvester Stallone plays a violent, late-twentieth-century cop thawed out of cryogenic prison by the wimps who pass for cops in a politically correct future. Meat-eating, hostility and carnal sex are forbidden (it's a girlish sort of fascism) and machines spew out fines whenever someone says a bad word. Unable to use the hi-tech toilets, Sly murmurs obscenities at one of these machines to get a good supply of paper.

Contrary to rumour, this is not how things actually work in Australian universities with equal opportunity language strategies and iffy plumbing. 'Speech codes' is an American term, much less of a mouthful than Australian bureaucracy's 'guidelines for the use of non-discriminatory language', but also a lot less accurate for our conditions. Codes can be compulsory, like road rules. Guidelines are not. Codes may formalise moral philosophies, guidelines make suggestions for how to get things done.

Call them what you will, they are not lists of bad words and they do not turn red-blooded men and women vegetarian. Let me talk about a real one, *Language Matters*—the 32-page brochure available from the Equal Opportunity Unit at UTS. It is not an obligatory or enforceable policy (unlike the 'house style' routinely imposed by newspaper editors and publishers). It is not used for fining or in any way punishing people. It does not outlaw hostility, ban prejudice, forbid hatred or censor opinion. It is not about preventing deliberate verbal abuse or speech inciting others to hatred (that is vilification, not discrimination).

Language Matters deals with problems that are far more common than overt conflict when a diverse group of strangers gets together for a limited, practical purpose, like taking a class. How do you talk politely to everyone at once when you haven't got a clue who they are? How can you avoid offending people unwittingly, when you don't know about their culture or their personal experience of life? How do you make everyone feel equally included, valued and able to participate—when the class itself is as likely to have tensions and hostilities as any other social group? How do you create enough tolerance in the room to let everyone get on with the job?

These problems may seem precious or trivial to people who don't spend their time working with strangers, or who think of universities as the cosy communities of old. They can actually be very destructive, not least because people falsely accused of having intended an insult feel humiliated in turn. They can also waste a lot of time. I once used the phrase 'calling a spade a spade' ten minutes into a talk in the United States, where I was taken as enthusiastically recommending the use of a derogatory word for a black person. I never did extricate myself or finish the talk, and while I learned an important lesson, I would rather have read it in a speech code.

Most of the advice in *Language Matters* is simple, or can seem so from the cosmopolitan, I've-been-around, some-of-my-best-friends-are perspective of many pundits who send up PC language. The truth is that many people new to university haven't 'been around' much at all, and that some staff spend most of their private lives without being around people like their students. I once had to learn the hard way—a testy public rebuke—that girls from Bankstown who don't look British or Irish tire of being asked where they're 'originally from' (to take one example from the brochure), and it is surprising how often people simply don't know that 'friendly insult' is not a universally understood custom, or a wise way to bond with a stranger.

Of course, if you want to insult strangers you are free to go ahead, although these days you are not entitled to expect that the person you insult will pretend not to be insulted.

The real problem is that we are all parochial to some extent now in relation to the complexity of our own society. Basically, guidelines like *Language Matters* give an etiquette for dealing with this situation—something social conservatives should approve. As a guide to good manners in the midst of diversity, *Language Matters* is more experimental, but much simpler, than the etiquettes of old which tried to produce uniformity. It boils down to four basic principles of politeness: don't harp about people's differences when it isn't necessary; do try to treat everyone equally and fairly; don't use euphemisms for disabilities or make jocular remarks to people you don't know about their race, their looks or their sexuality; do call people whatever they prefer to be called, and if you don't know, ask them.

In what sort of a society are these principles thought sinister or laughable? Not ours, I hope, especially since the last allows anyone who wants to be called a cripple rather than wheelchair-user, 'Australian' without an ethnic prefix, or Mrs rather than Ms, to have their wishes respected. Anti-PC crusaders who do find tolerance a joke have made mileage out of treating examples from workplace codes as though they were absolute rules of life: 'these lunatics want to ban "ladies"!' *Language Matters* does say, accurately, that 'women' is used more widely now than 'ladies' as a neutral term, but it also suggests that 'men' goes with 'women' and 'ladies' goes with 'gentlemen': to talk about 'men and ladies' may be fine in some contexts, but in a working environment it comes over as trivialising. However, if I want to be called a lady at work, a lady I can ask to be called.

Speech guidelines do not suggest euphemistic ways of talking about people but polite ways of talking *to* them—not piety behind the back but courtesy face to face. There is a difference. Robert Hughes may be right to say in *Culture of Complaint* that 'the usual American response to inequality is to rename it, in the hope that it will then go away'.[1] Perhaps Americans exist who say 'differently abled' with a straight face, though I have never seen it done; *Language Matters* gets all stern and finger-waggish about such phrases ('strongly discouraged'). But the point about sharing a workplace with people is that they do not go away, and they are neither named nor 'renamed' in their absence. Of course all the inequality in the world does not vanish when we encourage respect—it doesn't have to be love—in a classroom. But is that really a reason not to do it?

A more serious criticism, it seems to me, is that too much fuss about phrasing and names can make people feel like victims—frail petals in need of special linguistic delicacy of touch. Being rather partial myself to 'life-is-hard-get-used-to-it' moral fables, I am always ambivalent about this. How much fuss is too much fuss? There isn't any simple answer, because people are different. Glorifying toughness is no improvement on sanctified whining.

I do know that unthinking cruelty can devastate people already feeling frail. My own education was kinked for years by that early brush with late Menzies-era PC. I become an ardent writer but a furtive scholar, staying out late at night then studying until dawn so no one would know I did it (sluts don't swot), and by the time I made it to university I was terrified of talking out loud about books.

As a silent girl, I was treated as dumb by some of my

tutors. One accused me of plagiarism (of what he couldn't say) when he read my first essay; a dumb girl couldn't have written it. Another did something much worse for my confidence about talking out loud. One day, we were reading a scatological poem by Dryden. I was enjoying it, dreamily, when I heard him say: 'What does the lady in the green dress think? . . . *Does* the lady think?'

This is the sort of casual discriminatory gesture—not really meant to hurt, not thought out, not even malicious— that *Language Matters* asks us to imagine from the receiving end. When I looked up, there was a roomful of men (I think no other ladies were present) sniggering at my bright red face, and I knew they thought I was embarrassed by the bad words in the poem. Until then, I'd assumed I was one of the class, a student among students, getting used to the relentless demand of universities for fluency in speech. Suddenly I was a brainless outsider, a lady in a green dress caught reading dirty books.

There is nothing new in the idea of language reform. It is a fundamental tradition of Western civilisation; without it, Christianity would not have survived as a major religion, education would still be conducted in Latin, and democracy might have remained a loony radical idea. This does not mean that every reform is good, or that reformers ever get exactly what they want. Language is a collective product, and no one can control it or prevent it from changing.

PC language sets out to help us represent the social world the way it is now, not the way it was 30 years ago when most people in university seminars really were white men, give or take the odd white lady. In the process, it easily becomes coy, pedantic and prissy. But when it gets too absurd or fails to serve any useful purpose, people laugh, quarrel about it, criticise each other and come up with better ideas. Soon, someone will improve on 'person with paraplegia', and someone else will find an alternative to multiculturalism that will seize our imagination.

In the meanwhile, fussing a little bit about phrasing and names can actually help reduce the need for 'special delicacy' in talking together about important things. These are not always social or political issues. Even in universities, no one wants to turn every class into a workshop in personal tensions, and except in language, literature and media classes—a minuscule part of any university—most people do not want to spend their time poring over words. At UTS, much of the demand for *Language Matters* comes from people working in technical and practical fields who do not centre their lives on language—unlike those of us who fight about PC.[1]

Speech codes have no hope whatsoever of eradicating inequality and intolerance, and they fail dismally as brainwashing programs. But that is not what they are for. They help create spaces of temporary equality, working tolerance, in which everyone has a good chance to participate. The price of retreating from the effort to extend those spaces is one that almost all of us would have to pay.

Notes

1 Robert Hughes, *Culture of Complaint: The Fraying of America*, Oxford University Press, New York, 1993.
2 My thanks to Lyn Shoemark for explaining this to me.

Free speech, cheap talk and the Virtual Republic

BY MCKENZIE WARK

'I pity you. You're young white males at the turn of the twenty-first century and your time is past. I wouldn't be you for anything.' So says the diffident old professorial curmudgeon, just as he is about to be ousted from the Great Books course at Havenhurst College by a cabal of 'politically correct' students. But then, after the ad break, and after wallowing in a heady mix of burgundy, Beethoven and self-pity, he rallies, he takes them all on. Marching proudly into his class of surly students, he declares: 'Let the past argue with the future! That is the process. That has always been the process. This is all I have to offer.' While a few Blacks, Asians and women skulk, the rest give him a standing ovation, which he waves off in favour of a lecture on Rousseau.

* * *

A journalist returns to her *alma mater* to receive an honorary doctorate, and takes a film crew with her to record the event. The thing she looks forward to most is the chance to be filmed sitting in on a women's studies course. After all, as she needlessly reminds everyone more than once, she was one of the people who agitated for its creation in the first place. The class starts late. The teacher explains that punctuality is a kind of 'patriarchal dominance'. It's all downhill from there for famous journalist— the women in the class all find her loud, rude, abrasive, pushy—patriarchal, in a word. No matter what she does or says, they reject everything about her.

*   *   *

These sound like typical political correctness stories, of the kind that appear, vanish, and reappear in newspaper editorials. PC, in one form or another, is still with us, even though the government and the media have sternly proclaimed its death sentence. The notion—and, more importantly, what it implies—still needs debate, even though the topic has been taken off the boil.

The first of these stories is from a now defunct TV drama called 'Class of 96'. The second, from the TV sitcom 'Murphy Brown'. Yet when the rhetoric of PC was accused of being everywhere, actual documented cases were surprisingly thin on the ground. I sometimes wonder if PC was (is?) more fiction than fact. More people seemed to talk about David Williamson's play *Dead White Males*, or even David Mamet's play *Oleana*, as if these constituted evidence that the thing exists.

When editorialising about the perils of PC in the *Australian* even Williamson himself only offered one actual instance, and a second-hand one at that. He claimed that at a writer's conference in the 1980s someone showed him a checklist issued by the New Zealand Broadcasting Commission's drama department detailing 20 ways women are not to be depicted.[1] The accompanying picture showed Williamson as Gulliver, pegged to the ground, presumably by the Lilliput minds of PC. And yet, when I tried to write about Williamson's *Dead White Males* for the paper, the section editor was so concerned about libel that the review was 'legalled' by the paper's lawyer. The changes requested would have so diluted the point of the piece that there was no point in even trying. I was practically the only living Australian writer Williamson referred to in his various broadsides, and yet I was denied the chance to reply out of paranoia about libel and Williamson's alleged 'litigiousness'.

The facts about the origins of political correctness are not really in dispute. Some far right-wing foundations in the United States funded a series of books, campus publications, lecture tours and media campaigns to beat up the idea that the radical left were seizing hold of American campuses, and imposing rigid doctrines and dogmas of speech and thought. There is indeed a witch-hunt on American campuses. It is not being run by hard-left radicals hounding their conservative opponents, as fabled. It is the other way around. Conservatives are using the accusation that the left is too PC as an excuse to silence debate. Since the early 1990s, the American media has been only too ready to amplify such unsupported charges. The Australian media picked up and repeated these beat-ups *ad nauseam* without questioning the evidence. But there is no conspiracy of left-wing intellectuals to subvert the course of free inquiry in the United States. They simply do not have the numbers to do so, or the inclination. And yet this insidious little term 'PC' insinuated itself into our language.

'PC' was originally an expression used by tolerant left-of-centre American academics to sum up precisely the sort of attitude they tried to avoid. In Australia, the thing a sensible leftie would usually eschew is being too 'IS', or 'ideologically sound'. Those in Australian making the 'PC' charge transplanted the American 'PC' rhetoric and ignored the local 'IS' one. All the noise about PC in Australia was an echo of somebody else's axes grinding. It's a tribute to the lack of imagination of our intellectual Tories that they borrowed a gimmick as American as Coca-Cola rather than attempt to analyse our own intellectual culture in its own terms.

Then there's 'the new McCarthyism'. Like McCarthy's famous lists of Communist government officials, the evidence for PC is weak.

In 1991 the American Council for Education found 'little evidence of controversy over political correctness' on campus. Perhaps they forgot to survey Havenhurst. In Australia it would be hard to point to any instance where debate has actually been silenced on any social issue by the left. It has hardly ever been in a powerful enough position to do so. All that is ever asked is that the terms of debate not deliberately insult or inflame. As Triple J DJ Helen Razer put it, all that is really being asked is "the moral equivalent of leaving the room to break wind'.

I'm reminded of another talk-back radio personality, Stan Zemanek, who appeared on ABC TV's '7.30 Report', arguing against academic Mary Kalantzis and judge Pat O'Shane. They both know very well what happens on the street when the community's free-floating anxiety comes to rest on migrants or Aborigines for a moment, that for some people this may mean real acts of violence. It is everyone's right to cherish bigotry and ignorance, but it is common courtesy to express any view in a manner at least minimally couth.

I had first-hand experience of this back in the days when historian Geoffrey Blainey called into question levels of immigration, the numbers of Asian migrants, and the policy of multiculturalism. At the time I was in love with a fourth-generation Chinese Australian woman, and we would often walk down King Street in Newtown, Sydney, hand-in-hand, as people do. But after Blainey's remarks were televised, we were spat on, insulted, threatened with violence. I would strongly defend Blainey's right to speak his mind, and I am not accusing him of racism or even of direct responsibility for what might result from what he said. But I think any responsible public figure needs to consider such consequences when deciding on how to phrase their views, whatever those views may be.

For free speech to be an absolute right for any individual to say what they like, how they like, we must assume that what any individual says actually has no effect on the ability of others to speak effectively. If that were true there would be little point in actually exercising such a right in the first place. What may actually happen, however, is that an individual exercising that right to speak does affect the ability of others to speak, whether by simply taking up all the available time, by creating an atmosphere of prejudice preventing another view from being heard, or by configuring the space of debate such that it fails to recognise other points of view as legitimate.

To avoid such possibilities, to achieve free speech as the goal of the process as a whole, means that there are limits to the degree to which individual parties to a debate can exercise their right. The individual right to speak freely has to be recognised, in all cases, but it does not follow that it is absolute. This proposition was not often heard in the PC debate —not least because some of the proponents of an absolute right to free speech seek nonetheless to deny the legitimacy of any point of view which questions that right's absoluteness. The anti-PC pundits banged on relentlessly about an individual's absolute right to free speech—except if that individual denies that it is an absolute right. With defenders like that, free speech is hardly in need of enemies.

The notion that there was a campaign against the free exercise of individual speech came from a quite specific campaign in the American media against the academic left, particularly in the prestigious 'Ivy League' campuses. Allan Bloom might be credited with providing the first bit of intellectual backbone to this movement, with his high-minded book *The Closing of the American Mind*. The wilder claims of a left-wing 'McCarthyism' first surfaced in the fringe publications of the American right. A book called *An Illiberal Education* by former 'domestic policy analyst' for the Reagan administration Dinesh D'Souza padded it out.[2] It made headlines. Its claims have not stood up to scrutiny. *New Republic* magazine generously described it as 'an any-weapon-to-hand collection of slightly suspect anecdotes'.

Have we all forgotten what real McCarthyism was like? President Truman's 1947 order authorising the FBI to conduct loyalty checks of federal employees unleashed a witch-hunt from which American intellectual culture never recovered. The attacks on leftist and liberal intellectuals, conducted then as now in terms of a defence of 'free speech', led to the sacking of hundreds of faculty and government employees. Some, like mathematician Chandler Davis, went to prison rather than accept unconscionable attacks on civil liberties. Others, including literature scholar F. O. Mathiessen and historian E. H. Norman were driven to despair and suicide.[3]

In Australia, security checks on academics and writers were routine. In her book *Writers Defiled*, Fiona Capp showed how ASIO spied upon and harassed Australian writers. In *Writing in Hope and Fear*, John McLaren showed how security reports on the politics of authors and academics were used against them.[4] Some of Australia's most famous authors were denied financial support on purely political grounds. John Howard used the opportunity of what was supposed to be his answer in parliament to Independent MP Pauline Hanson to decry the 'sort of McCarthyism that was creeping into Australian politics under the former prime minister'.[5] But if ever there was a prince of McCarthyism and political correctness in Australia, it was the conservatives' hero, Robert Menzies.

If America's McCarthyite purge of the academy, the arts and the civil service was a genuine tragedy, then PC is a fantasy and a farce. It is difficult to find any comparable evidence of discrimination against conservatives today. Some of the most oft-cited cases in the US involved a little more than a questioning of the views of respected teachers by students from minority groups.

The most frequently cited case concerned Harvard historian Stephan Thernstrom and his course 'The Peopling of America'. Some of his students claimed that his teaching of southern plantation life was biased towards slave owner accounts, and that he was unresponsive to their criticisms.

They took their complaint up in the student newspaper. He continued to ignore them. They took it to the Harvard Committee on Race Relations. The Harvard administration, after some argy-bargy, upheld Thernstrom's academic freedom. It was Thernstrom himself who decided to respond to criticism of his course by simply not teaching it.

Far from a threat to 'free speech', what we have here is students exercising that very right. The students did not want their teacher silenced or his course banned. They simply had a difference of opinion and they felt Thernstrom was not listening to them, so they pursued the matter outside the classroom. Yet if you were to believe what many prominent news sources wrote about it, Thernstrom was a 'victim' of political correctness.

Another frequently cited case involved Nancy Stumhofer, an English professor at Pennsylvania State University, who asked for a production of Goya's painting of the Naked Maja to be removed from her classroom. Aha! Political correctness! So claimed the conservative pundit Paul Johnson. Even the liberal art critic Robert Hughes fell for this one. He blamed it on 'academic thought police' from feminism's 'repressive fringe'.[6] But did Stumhofer really think the painting was 'sexually harassing' her? According to Stumhofer herself, she wanted the painting moved because when she tried to teach developmental English classes while standing in front of it, she could hear the students laughing and making remarks to each other, while looking past her at something on the wall. Far from having the painting 'censored', she asked for it to be removed to a more public part of the building than her classroom. The issue here really is not censorship, merely the appropriateness of certain contexts for displaying a nude.

Even the relatively trivial cases of PC in action that conservatives—and a few gullible liberals—made so much of often don't stand up to close scrutiny. Meanwhile, conservatives mounted vociferous attacks on free expression in the arts, such as the obscenity charge against Robert Mapplethorpe's photographs and the campaign against the National Endowment for the Arts.[7] Conservative academics and culture workers certainly did not lose their jobs. They were not being silenced or suppressed. They were merely being asked to explain themselves.

When conservative students complained about a black education professor at the University of Chicago and called for his removal, the national press was not moved to comment. Nor did we hear about the complaint taken up against Stumhofer by a conservative colleague and a maintenance worker when she distributed parts of John Berger's *Ways of Seeing* that contained reproductions of nudes. Or that Joe Rabinowitz, new director of the Fox network station in Washington, wrote a memo to the chair of Fox urging the firing of 'politically correct' employees. These stories don't fit the myth of political correctness as conservative cultural activists have crafted it and as the media has come to believe it.

Like any good propaganda, the PC farce took an atom of truth and made a bomb out of it. Yes, there are strident, vocal minorities of students on some American campuses who tenaciously cling to some desiderata of moral and political rectitude. Is that anything new? And yes, on some campuses students organise to undermine the authority—and authoritarianism—of disliked teachers. And so, in David Mammet's *Oleanna*, an academic is successfully rolled by a student on a charge of 'harassment' of which he is most likely innocent. Why is it that nobody produces plays with the opposite and more common scenario: academic does indeed harass student and gets away with it, because the student is too scared to act? The 'Class of 96' episode, *Oleanna* and Helen Garner's version of the Ormond College case in *The First Stone* have this in common with the whole rhetoric of PC: it is nearly always about the big white bloke. He is always the centre of the story. Even Williamson's play, which seems at first to be about the young woman student, is really about defending her actual and spiritual father figures from the attacks of the cultural studies teacher Swain and that awful feminist relative.

All of the famous cases of alleged 'political correctness' on American campuses are studied in some detail by John K. Wilson in his useful book, *The Myth of Policital Correctness*, published by the reputable academic house of Duke University Press.[8] As Wilson wrote, in 1991, '... PC went from an obscure phrase spoken by campus conservatives to a nationally recognised sound bit used to attack political dissenters on the left'. An earlier campaign by the right-wing group Accuracy in Academia that was based on spying on left-wing academics failed, being too clearly McCarthyite and in breach of the principles of academic freedom. But with the PC campaign, 'The conservatives gain a major strategic victory when they declared themselves to be the oppressed ....'.

'Without the support of liberals, the conservatives' attacks would have been dismissed as the same old complaints ...', wrote Wilson. So they dressed up a conservative attack on the left as a campaign for free speech and civil rights. This had even otherwise astute and liberally minded souls like Robert Hughes singing the PC tune, not to mention the fictional character of Murphy Brown. Particularly successful was the appeal to the resentment among journalists and the public of the supposedly privileged life of higher education.

The campaign against PC was initiated by far-right-wing think-tanks with a great deal more money than credibility. Allen Bloom and Dinesh D'Souza both received money from the Olin Foundation. These PC myth-makers are not defending free speech, they are practicing bought speech.[9] Richard Bernstein, who wrote an infamous *New York Times* beat-up, thanked the Bradley and the Smith-Richardson Foundations 'for making my research possible'.

What is truly disturbing is that while the news media prides itself on accuracy and fact-checking, a handful of incidents that are open to a range of interpretations were blown up out of all proportions into the myth of political correctness. A few instances of alleged left-wing PC have received all of the media attention, while persistent attacks on the left received practically none. While there may be room for debate on campus sexual conduct codes and the definition of rape, the celebrated examples all come from liberal colleges. The draconian standards applied to both faculty and student behaviour at many religious educational institutions is not criticised by conservatives.

So this was the context for the PC rhetoric that was so enthusiastically imported into Australia. As in America, what began as a conservative attack on the humanities academy quickly found friends among vaguely left-of-centre figures nursing their own grievances against changes afoot in academic culture since 'their day'. The enormous expansion of higher education under the Hawke and

Keating governments shifted the centre of gravity within Australian culture. Never before had so many Australians passed through the classrooms of the humanities. Never before had it seemed so essential to get a degree to get a job.

So there are two sources of resentment of the academy. One is those branches of the culture elites who feel they are losing their authority—particularly the old Whitlam ascendency of writers and artists who benefited from a previous government's largess in the arts but who are no longer the last word in intellectual sophistication. Compared to the newly expanded academy, however, they have pretty good access to the mainstream media. The other source of resentment is students themselves. The government expanded the numbers in higher education far more than the money—students found themselves crammed into classrooms for what often seemed like a meaningless paper chase. The academic in Mamet's *Oleanna* quite rightly calls this the 'warehousing' of a generation, only he is too full of himself to explain this to his student in a way that doesn't seem patronising or offensive to her.

Both Williamson's play and Helen Garner's book *The First Stone* were pretty popular with students, these being among the few well-promoted reflections on campus life to make their way through the geriatric arteries of the contemporary media sphere.[10] Both appear to be about raising the alarm concerning new movements in the humanities academy such as an excessively moralising feminism. Both see the new breed of academics as cynical and manipulative in their attempt to seize hold of students minds. From talking to my own students, many of them took to both the book and the play with enthusiasm but tended to find them both patronising. I don't know about anyone else's students, but mine seem pretty keen and able to think for themselves and filter out the views of their teachers. The irony of course is that if one teaches students to be critical, then they are going to be critical—of what you or anyone else tries to teach them. It didn't take them long and required absolutely no prompting from me for them to ask after Garner and Williamstown's own claims to authority, their own appeal for the hearts and minds of the young. If Garner and Williamson offered cynical readings of the attempts to indoctrinate a generation in PC ways, then my students at least were just as capable of a cynical reading of Garner and Williamson's texts as cynical attempts to bolster their own flagging influence.

Neither text gels much with my own experience either, although I too have my criticisms, not of Australian academic PC but of certain currents of thought that left themselves open to such a tactic. In the early 1980s I volunteered for courses in women's studies, taught by Judith Allen and Rosemary Pringle and Vivien Johnson. I was often the only male in class. Judith's classes took place in her office. Maybe nine or ten people, jammed into a tiny room. Rosemary's classes were a bit more relaxed—I think we even sat on bean bags, stewn across the floor. It was a very seventies kind of thing. She was writing about women in the workforce at the time—detailed studies of what actually happens in a whitegoods factory or a bank. Or I remember Vivien lecturing on women's refuges—she was involved in the movement to set them up and subsequently wrote a book about it. I remember a rather diminutive woman smoking Marlboros and talking about women turning up bruised and battered, scared to death of their own husbands.

At first I found it a bit intimidating. A lot of the women in the classes were mature-age students. They had kids my age. They had come back to university to get the education they missed out on when they chose to raise a family. Or there were younger women, often very energetically committed to the cause, as young people sometimes are. I found it prudent to just listen for a while, rather than barge on in like I usually did. And do you know what? I learned something. Something about other people's perceptions of the world; other people's way of refining and sharpening those perceptions against the stone of sociology, history or philosophy.

I didn't necessarily agree with everything. A writer by the name of Mary Daly was popular at the time. Daly was a Catholic theologian-turned-feminist whose project included the creation of a distinctive women's language. This seemed to me to be informed as much by some kind of quaint, 1970s hippie sensibility as anything distinctively female. It seemed to lead its adherents into assuming that there was some natural difference in the way women thought and talked and wrote, without such an assumption being really tested. It seemed to confuse the proposition that there ought to be a separate domain of women's language, with the proposition that there is such a thing—two quite different kinds of statement.

Anyway, there were some pretty lively exchanges about Mary Daly in those days. French feminist authors, with a somewhat less hippy-dippy style of women's writing, would come along later and take her place in that particular project, but at that particular moment, Daly was all the rage. I could see why there might be something in the idea of separatism. If women are to put in words their own feelings and thoughts and perspectives on the world, then it seemed a valid option to me that some women might want to separate themselves from being wives and nursemaids and concentrate on living with each other. But I could also see that this could lead to the creation of a kind of group-think where everyone was obliged to agree with each other, where women who didn't get with the program would be ostracised, where the beliefs and practices of the group would drift away from what women in everyday life thought and felt. I wasn't alone in having such reservations. Some women were a bit wary about it all too. The difference was, of course, that I wasn't a woman, and here I was writing assignments on these controversial issues that were going to be marked by feminists.

I got lower grades for my feminism courses in my final year than for anything else. Outrageous! Discrimination! I thought about lodging appeals, taking them on. But then I thought about it some more. In the first place, I really wasn't as well read in this stuff as the other students. I was busy reading other things. I simply didn't have the first-hand experience of the issues that some of the better students in these classes had. Should that matter? Surely university should be a level playing field! But the problem with that argument is that for some of these women, it wasn't a level playing field at all. Running a household for a husband and raising kids was what they knew most about. They felt disadvantaged in other courses, that dealt with things they had to read about in books to catch up with. Here were one or two courses that dealt with their experience of the world, its history or its place in the contemporary world. No wonder they did well in such courses. Women's studies was their home base in the humanities, the place where they were sure they knew what they were on about, where they got the confidence to tackle other issues. For me, it was the other way around. I was expecting to do well in it because I knew I was pretty up on criminology or contemporary politics or whatever.

In my whole time as an undergraduate I never once felt that the moral or political pressure coming from other students or from teachers shut me up. There were some pretty strongly held views, both among the staff and the students. It could be fairly intimidating. But then, to some extent it was supposed to be. The humanities and the social sciences, among other things, teach you how to argue. How to find relevant facts. How to choose and apply a relevant interpretive framework. What the known weaknesses of other propositions are and how to go after them. Not everyone got into the classroom hurly-burly. But some of the quiet ones, I discovered, were the ones turning in first-rate written assignments. They were the people to seek out and share notes with over a quiet coffee. Some were just not very interested. I know the humanities and social sciences are supposed to be 'Mickey Mouse' courses—the kind few people actually fail. But they are also courses in which few people really excel.

I certainly knew a few ideologues as an undergraduate, and very occasionally I get them now in my classes. Such people have always been around. Militants and godbotherers, missionaries and thought police. They are not a new creation. Read Manning Clark's memoirs of his education, *The Quest for Grace*, and they are there. 'Heart dimmers' and 'life deniers', he called them—both better expressions than that clumsy import, PC. As Clark used to say, real believers don't need to make the world conform to their needs. They are strong enough to endure a world that thinks and acts otherwise. I've had some lively and illuminating conversations with true believers, with Moslems, Communists, Catholic priests. I supervised a thesis once on the relationship between Moslem faith and enlightenment as both pertained to a practice of broadcasting for a Moslem country. Or another, on how the West uses human rights as a propaganda strategy against China, as seen by a very bright young Chinese apparatchik. We had some fine old arguments, but precisely because of a lack of anxiety about whether the process would challenge anyone's belief.

I've also supervised work that has challenged a student's whole identity—those can be dangerous. Real knowledge is threatening. It changes you. I've had students come to see me and burst into tears, dissolving in a puddle on my office floor—not just from the ordinary working pressure of getting a course finished, but because they really feel in danger of losing a sense of self, of becoming someone else. I see my role in such a metamorphosis as supporting the person who wants to grow, intellectually. I don't push in any particular direction, although actually I think it's easier sometimes for students with supervisors who do push in a particular direction. It gives them a much clearer goal to either head towards or resist.

One hardly ever hears about such things in the media. How is it that while so many people now experience higher education and all the frustrations and anxieties that go with it, so little is said about it—from the student's point of view? Thankfully, the movie *Love and Other Catastrophes* finally put at least one version of the experience into circulation that takes into account the student point of view. For the most part, it's the resentments of outsiders that get the attention. The university has become a favourite imaginary site for two branches of the public sphere pushed a bit off-axis by expanded higher education to vent a bit of spleen—the Whitlam ascendancy in the arts and what's left of journalism in the declining circulations of the quality press. In this case it's an old bit of splenetic juice— the intellectual as threat to good order—and it comes in two flavours. Intellectuals are immoral postmodern sceptics who believe in nothing but power and will do anything to manipulate it to further their own nihilistic ends; intellectuals are moral fanatics who believe in rigid and austere dogmas that deny people free expression and rob them of their enjoyment of harmless everyday bits of fun. The first accusation is an old one; the second is curious. It's what people used to say about the priests. Perhaps its symptomatic of the decline of religion in our relentlessly secular public life that the blame gets shifted from the excessive moral authority of the church to that of the university-bred intellectuals.

I think resistance to moral authoritarianism is always a healthy thing. Only in this case it seems to be a massive simulation exercise. Phantom armies of elitist zealots are conjured out of a few dubious anecdotes as a pretext for staging popular resistance to them. To the extent that this affirms the democratic and secular nature of ethical thought and practice in Australia, fine. Only as we've seen, it's not quite so simple. I do wish some of the feverish campaigners against PC would get off their bums and become equally feverish about the kind of free speech they are encouraging to come out of the woodwork. Where are they, now that they've provided the covering fire for

Pauline Hanson, or for Port Lincoln Mayor Peter Davis, who thinks, and feels confident stating publicly, that 'if you are a child of a mixed race, particularly, if you will, Asian-Caucasian or Aboriginal-white, you are a mongrel and that's what happens when you cross dogs or whatever'?[11] I am of course quite happy to defend Peter Davis's right to call people mongrels, and feel free to exercise my right to call Peter Davis an asshole.

This may be 'free' speech, in that a few people get the odd inflammatory insult in edgeways, but it isn't dialogue. It isn't free speech in the larger sense of enabling people to engage each other in discussion, in spite of differences, through the observance of some formal constraints on ways of speaking. If there was a project going on in the humanities departments within universities, it was a debate about what kinds of protocols of speech might free speech to express a wider range of views on a wider range of topics than is currently the case in the public sphere in Australia. That project brought together people whose roots were in feminism, multiculturalism, Aboriginal cultural activism and much else besides. It was a vast and amorphous movement, part of which one can identify as Australian cultural studies.[12]

I was part of that project—I went to its conferences, published in its journals, engaged in some of its debates. If there was a common aim to cultural studies, it appears to me to be one of firstly inquiring into the conditions of possibility for a truly diverse and democratic culture, and secondly of conducting some modest experiments towards actually practicing cultural studies as if it were trying to be such a thing, already. Cultural studies had at least three moments. The first was the discovery of just how different the experiences of Australians actually are and always were, for example the hidden histories of women's or migrants' experiences. The second was the criticism of cultural institutions that had ignored or suppressed particular cultural values of aspirations, for example the forced adoption of Aboriginal children and the imposition of mission religion. The third moment was the positive attempt to imagine how Australian culture could be otherwise—how might free, open, diverse, creative, tolerant culture come about?

The irony is that such a project tended to operate with too narrow an understanding of cultural difference. It left some of the older and deeper cultural currents out of the picture. It assumed there was a strong and central 'dominant' culture of big white blokes that would take care of itself. But there isn't. The irony is that a 'dominant white culture' was kept in place by the very attempts to find an alternative to it. The ways of speaking that proliferated in the humanities were more conservative than they knew. They took for granted something that was already fragmented and increasingly isolated from the drift of the various proposals for the further reform of manners of speaking.

Sure one can find racist and sexist stereotypes in the media, and all that. But one can also find quite the opposite. Feminism and multicuralism are now part of popular culture. They have not abolished their nemeses, and probably never will. But pick up any popular women's magazine and you will find articles with a feminist bent sandwiched in between diet tips and fashion. That's the very real diversity of the public sphere. I truly believe that, certain set backs and reactions not withstanding, the tendency is towards a more liberal and enlightened media, provided people are prepared to roll up their sleeves and get into it and fight the good fight.

Cultural studies tended to get stuck at each of the steps along the way. Sometimes the discovery of cultural difference seemed to be an end in itself. Sometimes the critique of the allegedly dominant culture would eclipse all attempts to move the agenda on to positive developments elsewhere. Sometimes the notion of a positive process of creating a diverse culture got too obsessed with cultural policy, looking for administrative ways around the unavoidable need to engage with cultural change where it really happens—through popular culture and the media.

In overestimating the power and homogeneity of the 'dominant discourse', cultural studies sometimes treated the big white bloke way of talking as the universal media model of public speech at precisely the time when it was no longer quite so. The media are still pretty full of big white blokes who are still pretty full of themselves. But they are already sharing the public sphere with enough other voices to call into question the idea that the big white bloke way of saying and doing things is somehow natural and inevitable. Cultural studies participated in the fantasy of the very thing most of its practitioners wanted to displace.

I had some fun moments, particularly at cultural studies conferences, negotiating a place in which to speak in these brave new experiments. It wasn't impossible. I think it was a good thing for a nice middle-class white boy like me to have to think a bit before opening my mouth. Rather than everyone who didn't quite fit in having to find a place and a way to speak, it was a bit the other way around. Can't say it ever stopped me. But it made me pause and think. It's no accident that my first book was about how the international impinges on all this, how the global flows of news media interact and intersect with local cultural differences and frictions. It seemed like the right kind of topic for a white bloke to write about.

When the PC stuff started to come up, it seemed obvious to me that here was an example of what I had found in those studies. Images and stories that arose out of a specific conflict, transported across national borders, being used to articulate quite other conflicts. In this case, PC as the American right's bludgeoning of the campus left transported through the ether to Australia, where PC became the vehicle for the Whitlam ascendancy in the arts and conservative pundits in the papers to attack the expanding universities and check the possible expansion of their influence.

Meanwhile cultural studies continued on its merry way, asking questions; finding new ways of creating spaces for people to speak; working particularly on the most intractable problem in Australian culture—finding ways to have a dialogue with Aboriginal people. I can't remember a single major cultural studies conference that didn't put Aboriginal speakers in the plenary. But the small world of the humanities academy is only one of the worlds in which people may find themselves speaking. Not many scholars are all that media-savvy. Nobody took much trouble to explain what was going on. So when someone like David Williamson took a peek at a few frankly pretty second-rate textbooks and crib sheets for undergraduates, alarm bells went off. What was in the main an experiment in creating new, additional ways of speaking was taken to be some Machiavellian plan to design and impose a replacement. Neither Williamson nor anyone else has ever provided much evidence, but nevertheless the myth got about.

Irony of ironies, by organising themselves negatively against the pole of the big bad other—big white bloke talk—these experiments provided some legitimacy for the remnants of precisely that, at a time when people in public life who still felt helpless without such props were getting few and far between and feeling pretty vulnerable. About all that's been keeping rampant Anglo hetero masculine posturing together in public life is the relentless insistence of its few remaining devotees that someone is out to get them. Had such a myth never get out, such a mode of speech might have quietly passed on. Had cultural studies not made such a fetish of it, there might never have been much to make such a hysterical reaction out of in the first place.

A further consequence of the success of the campaign against PC is that it has given licence for precisely the kinds of resentment and confusion lurking in the bits and pieces of what was once a dominant white discourse that one hears from Pauline Hanson or Graeme Campbell. Cultural studies has been very good at identifying the hidden injuries of race and gender, and finding ways within the academy to articulate those grievances, to have them heard. But it hasn't been so good at the hidden injuries of class. At a time when the globalisation and rationalisation and every other top-down euphemisation for the reorganisation of Australia was being made to suit the banks and big business, it escaped a lot of people's attention that there were sections of the community who were—and are—really hurting. Working people who find their skills are no longer up to scratch, small businesses squeezed out by the big franchises, farmers watching their credit and their markets dry up quicker than a river in drought.

At the end of the day, I think the issue is still one of discovering how different people's cultural life can be, of finding what limits its expression and free development, of creating arenas where diversity can thrive and yet maintain a dialogue, a sense of a collective project. A culture that can produce, side by side, the novels of Justine Ettler, the plays of David Williamson, the poems of Les Murray, and the music of Yothu Yindi, and 'Full Frontal' on TV can't be all bad.

The attacks on PC, whether by David Williamson, Graeme Campbell, or John Howard have one thing in common. They all employ a paranoid way of thinking, according to which there is always a hidden evil lurking in our culture that threatens our way of life. They commandeer our attention, and prop up their own authority, by claiming to identify this menace. They are just like Joe McCarthy and the old cold warriors, who made a space for themselves in public life by claiming to find reds under every bed. They propose the eradication of this alleged threat as the panacea for all our cultural anxieties.

But they are not part of the cure, they are part of the problem. The only thing we have to fear is that anyone might take these fears too seriously. That there are tensions, differences, difficulties in negotiating our way through life in our mongrel culture is something to celebrate, make a few jokes about, and get down to working out in a sensible fashion. The goal is an Australia that conducts itself as a public conversation in which one way or another, in one place or another, every kind of speech can be heard, and in which everyone is enjoined to accept responsibility for finding a way to listen. This is something ordinary Australians usually do pretty well, at least when not disturbed by fearmongers. We can be genuinely curious, empathetic and engaged by our own multiplicity as a people. The popular tradition of the yarn, whether told over the back fence or down the pub, is about nothing else. Australians can be so good at cultural difference that we can even lend an ear to paranoid stories, be they tall, shaggy, second or third hand, or a covert party political broadcast. This is why I don't think, in the long run, that the cheap talk about PC gets anyone at all close to the heart of Australian culture. To me that will always be a slightly rowdy but good-natured bunfight in which people demand to have a fair go at proposing just exactly what a fair go might be. That's what I call the virtual republic, and its going on, virtually everywhere, even as we speak.

Notes

1 David Williamson, 'Truce in the Identity Wars', *Weekend Australian*, 11 May 1996; see also 'Universal Moral Soldier', *The Bulletin*, 2 April 1996.

2 Allan Bloom, *The Closing of the American Mind*, Simon & Schuster, New York, 1987; Dinesh D'Souza, *An Illiberal Education: The Politics of Race and Sex on Campus*, Vintage Books, New York, 1992.

3 See, for example, Victor Navasky, *Naming Names*, John Caldor, London, 1982. The story of E. H. Norman is told in John W. Dower's poignant introduction to E. H. Norman, *Origins of the Modern Japanese State*, Pantheon, Random House, New York, 1975. The story of just how damaging the McCarthyite witch-hunt among Asian studies scholars was to America's ability to think through its foreign policy in Asia, especially in Vietnam, is told in David Halberstam, *The Best and the Brightest*, Penguin Books, Harmondsworth, 1972.

4 Fiona Capp, *Writers Defiled*, McPhee Gribble, Melbourne, 1993;

John McLaren, *Writing in Hope and Fear: Literature as Politics in Postwar Australia*, Cambridge University Press, Melbourne, 1996.

5 John Howard, 'Tolerance a Part of Policy', *Australian*, 9 October 1996.

6 Robert Hughes, *Culture of Complaint: The Fraying of America*, Oxford University Press, New York, 1993, p. 30; for another view, see Nadine Strossen, *Defending Pornography: Free Speech, Sex, and the Fight for Women's Rights*, Scribner, New York, 1995; and the person heard from least in the mainstream reporting of this one—Stumhoffer herself: 'Goya's Naked Maja and the Classroom Climate', *Democratic Culture*, Spring 1994.

7 Wendy Steiner, *The Scandal of Pleasure: Art in the Age of Fundamentalism*, Chicago University Press, Chicago, 1995.

8 John K. Wilson, *The Myth of Political Correctness: The Conservative Attack on Higher Education*, Duke University Press, Durham, 1995 also of interest is Michael Bérube, *Public Access: Literary Theory and American Cultural Politics*, Verso, New York, 1994.

9 See McKenzie Wark, 'The Anti-Public Sphere', *21C: The Magazine of the 21st Century*, No. 2, 1995.

10 Helen Garner, *The First Stone*, Picador, Sydney, 1995; David Williamson, *Dead White Males*, Currency Press, Sydney, 1995.

11 Peter Davis, 'Mayor's Mongrels Claim Leaves Him In A Council of One', *Australian*, 23 October 1996.

12 See John Frow and Meaghan Morris, *Australian Cultural Studies: A Reader*, Allen & Unwin, Sydney, 1993.

About the authors

Phillip Adams is not to be confused with Padraic McGuinness, another black-garbed, bearded and rapidly crumbling columnist. Over the past 40 years, Adams has written countless millions of words for everything from Melbourne's *Communist Guardian* to London's *Sunday Times*. Employed by various media tycoons to demonstrate pluralism in their publications, he has also produced many feature films and documentaries, and he's chaired a wide range of organisations, including the Australian Film Commission, the Australian Film Institute and the Commission for the Future. Realising that the political tide was turning, he recently applied for, and was granted, political asylum at Radio National, where he presents 'Late Night Live'.

John Buchanan is the Deputy Director of the Australian Centre for Industrial Relations Research and Training (ACIRRT) at the University of Sydney. Prior to this he was Director of Policy Research in the Commonwealth Department of Industrial Relations in Canberra. He has degrees in history and law, and holds a diploma in economics. Between 1988 and 1991, Buchanan was part of the team that conducted the first comprehensive survey of workplace industrial relations in Australia, involving interviews with management and union representatives at over 2300 workplaces. He frequently comments on industrial relations issues on radio and television.

Bill Cope was, until August 1996, First Assistant Secretary in the Department of the Prime Minister and Cabinet and Director of the Office of Multicultural Affairs. Before that, he was Research Manager and then Director of the Centre for Workplace Communication and Culture at the University of Technology, Sydney, and James Cook University of North Queensland, a position to which he returned at the end of 1996. His most recent book is *Productive Diversity*, authored jointly with Mary Kalantzis.

Mary Kalantzis is Professor of Education at James Cook University of North Queensland and Director of the Institute of Interdisciplinary Studies. She is a part-time Commissioner of the Human Rights and Equal Opportunity Commission and Chair of the Queensland Ethnic Affairs Ministerial Advisory Committee, whose role is to advise the Premier on all matters relating to multiculturalism. Her publications include co-authorship of *Mistaken Identity: Multiculturalism and the Demise of Nationalism* (with Castles, Cope and Morrissey); *Minority Languages and Dominant Culture* (with Cope and Slade); *Cultures of Schooling: Pedagogies for Cultural Difference and Social Access* (with Cope, Noble and Ponting) and *Productive Diversity*.

Marcia Langton is Ranger Chair of Aboriginal and Torres Strait Islander Studies at Northern Territory University and Director of the Centre for Indigenous Natural and Cultural Resource Management. She is in her third term as Chair of the Council of the Australian Institute of Aboriginal and Torres Strait Islander Studies, and a member of the Aboriginal Reconciliation Council. Professor Langton has worked for three of the major Aboriginal land councils, the Royal Commission into Aboriginal Deaths in Custody, and is in great demand to lecture, publish and comment on contemporary social issues in Aboriginal affairs. She was awarded an AM in 1993 for services to anthropology and advocacy of Aboriginal rights.

Catharine Lumby is a lecturer in media studies at Macquarie University and a regular opinion columnist for the Sydney Morning Herald. She is the author of *Bad Girls: the Media, Sex and Feminism in the '90s*.

David Marr grew up in Sydney, studied law and became a journalist. Between stints on the *Bulletin*, the *National Times*, and 'Four Corners', he wrote biographies of Sir Garfield Barwick and Patrick White. In the last few years he has edited White's letters, presented ABC Radio National's 'Arts Today' and written for the *Sydney Morning Herald*.

Meaghan Morris is the Chair of the Human Rights Council of Australia. She holds an Australian Research Council Senior Fellowship at the University of Technology, Sydney, to write a book about the Australian journalist and writer, Ernestine Hill. She first heard about the UTS 'speech code' from a story on '60 Minutes', which gave her the idea that her UTS colleagues were lunatics trying to ban 'ladies'. Having spent 20 years writing about Australian film and television, she should have known better.

McKenzie Wark is the author of *Virtual Geography* (Indiana University Press) and *Virtual Republic* (Allen & Unwin), and a columnist for the *Australian*. He lectures in media studies at Macquarie University. He describes himself as a 'lapsed marxist in the pay of Rupert Murdoch'.